LOST
BATTLEFIELDS
OF BRITAIN

MARTIN HACKETT

To Jan & Paul

The Bakehouse is perfect a place
to stay as there could be
thank you

SUTTON PUBLISHING

First published in the United Kingdom in 2005 by
Sutton Publishing Limited · Phoenix Mill
Thrupp · Stroud · Gloucestershire · GL5 2BU

British Library Cataloguing in Publication Data
A catalogue record for this book is available from the British Library.

ISBN 0 7509 4170 7

Endpapers, front: The Severn valley at Welshpool; *rear*: Re-enactment of Montrose's
men's initial salvo at the battle of Inverlochy.

Typeset in 11.5/15pt Garamond 3.
Typesetting and origination by
Sutton Publishing Limited.
Printed and bound in England by
J.H. Haynes & Co. Ltd, Sparkford.

Contents

General Touring Information   v

Acknowledgements   ix

Map of Great Britain Showing the Battle Sites   xiii

Introduction   xiv

1   *Buttington – 893*   1

2   *St Albans – 22 May 1455*   17

3   *Norwich – 27 August 1549*   31

4   *Powick Bridge – 23 September 1642*   51

5   *Lyme – 20 April to 15 June 1644*   67

6   *Montgomery – 18 September 1644*   83

7   *Inverlochy – 2 February 1645*   99

8   *Stow-on-the-Wold – 21 March 1646*   115

9   *Killiecrankie – 27 July 1689*   129

10   *Goudhurst – 21 April 1747*   147

Bibliography   163

Index   167

General Touring Information

The author has personally visited and photographed, during the last twelve months, each battle site listed within this book, so that the information you read and the photographs you see should be as accurate and as up-to-date as possible; those photographs without a specific credit were all taken by the author. The majority of the photographs were taken during the winter months, so be prepared for some fields to look different if they are rich with crops where once bare soil lay; similarly with hedges and trees, their natural spring and summer growth may now obscure some landmarks that were clearly visible before, so be prepared for things to look a little different. Also the land use, infrastructure, road systems and rights of way can all change, sometimes at very short notice. If you encounter difficulties in following any tour then we would very much like to hear about it, so that we can incorporate changes in future editions. Your comments should be sent to the publisher at the address provided at the front of this book. With each battle is a scale map designed to illustrate the key locations on the tour and, where applicable, the key points are cross-referenced to the text. So that you derive maximum value and enjoyment from your exploration of these battle sites, I would suggest that you equip yourself with the following items:

- Appropriate maps. A general road map to navigate to the appropriate location and, if more detail is required, then either the Landranger or Explorer series of maps from the Ordnance Survey, which are available from all good booksellers in most high streets of the UK.
- Lightweight waterproof clothing and robust footwear. These are essential, especially if one leaves the footpaths of built-up areas.
- A compass. This is always a useful tool, and it allows the reader to verify the locations of troops and their movements upon the battlefield.
- A camera and spare films. The author always carries a cheap, disposable camera as emergency cover for his more expensive equipment, and they have saved the day on more than one occasion.

- A notebook to record details of any photograph taken and to jot down any changes that have occurred, with any information that you feel would be useful to the publishers.
- Food and drink. Although in Britain, in theory, you are never far from a retail outlet, there are roads in Wales and Scotland where, even in the twenty-first century, passing another car can be a rarity, especially in winter. It is therefore sensible always to take spare drinking water with you and some light refreshments, particularly if you are planning to do some of the full-length walks.
- Binoculars. An excellent aid especially when verifying the location and interpreting how much each army could have seen of the other when they were deploying for battle.

The author has visited all of the sites by vehicle as not all of them are accessible by rail, but in each chapter the details of the nearest railway station have been provided so that travellers can make their own arrangements if they intend to visit by train. Within each chapter are details on other attractions to see in the area, but this is not a definitive list; as the reader will appreciate, whole brochures are available on some towns and cities and it would be impossible to include every attraction or indeed cater for every taste. The author would advise anyone planning to visit any of these sites to contact the local tourist office, as they can provide news of any special events and are generally happy to post out information, including maps and places with accommodation. The author has contacted or visited over forty tourist offices in the last year and has received excellent service from all of them. To assist the reader, each chapter has the details for the local tourist office included.

For those disabled visitors wishing to visit a battle site, please take note of the routes and location points detailed. While it may not be possible to explore a complete site because of the nature of the terrain, wherever practicable the author has given vantage points, many of which can be reached by road. So, depending on the level of disability, the visitor should still be able to enjoy the majority of locations within the book. Buttington, St Albans, Norwich, Powick Bridge, Lyme, Montgomery, Stow and Goudhurst all fall into this category, while some parts of both Inverlochy and Killiecrankie could also be visited.

SOME DOS AND DON'TS

Touring a battlefield can be an interesting, a rewarding and sometimes a most emotional experience, especially if you have studied the battle beforehand or are related to people who were involved in it. However, it is clear from my tours that although there are some locals who know that a battle was fought in their area, there will also be people who are totally unaware that there was any kind of military action there, so be patient if you are quizzed and simply explain the reason for your interest in the location.

Wherever possible, all of the routes are on the public highway, along public footpaths and bridleways, or across other recognised footpaths – a harbour wall for example. Therefore, when walking, please keep to these designated rights of way, but if you do stray and you are asked to leave the land you are on, then please do so immediately by the quickest and safest way possible. Particularly in Scotland, keep to the designated paths; there are bogs and ditches that lie unseen, covered by layers of moss and heather which can cause injury if one is unlucky enough to step down into one.

Always be aware, especially in rural areas, of not blocking gates or drives to farms when choosing a place to park. If you take a dog with you, and Rosie accompanied the author on all of his walks without any problem, remember that there are times when the dog must be on the lead both in the town and the country; this is for both the dog's safety and that of wildlife and farm animals. If there is no clear parking place, then choose an open stretch of road where vehicles coming from both directions can clearly see your position. If you have to use a gate to continue your walk, then please ensure that the gate is closed, and secured behind you, before you move on.

Do not feed animals that you find on the walks: it is dangerous to the animal and potentially dangerous to the person providing the food, as these are wild animals, not domesticated pets. The owner of one estate upon which a battle site encroaches was fortunate enough to see and stop a woman feeding crisps to one of her Highland cows; the woman was pleased that the cow appreciated the crisps sufficiently to nuzzle his 24in pointed horns up the side of her head and face, unaware that a sudden move could have led to her being blinded or gored.

Many country estates have shoots or equestrian events and, although the author is not aware that any battle sites in this book are near such an estate, as stated above, things change. Therefore if you hear gunshots, or there are signs indicating that there is a shoot or a cross-country event in progress, make sure that you are on the correct route and, if unsure, try and verify with the local farmer or landowner where the event is taking place and what walks will be affected.

Finally, as one sometimes reads in the press, it happens that someone may find a small artefact: a ring, a coin or perhaps a cannon ball. If you find any artefacts upon the battle site, then if possible leave them where they are and mark their location with a stone or stick, and then photograph a landmark in relation to the object so that the marker can be found; use a Global Positioning System instrument if you have one. Then contact the landowner and the local police, who will be able to put you in touch with the relevant archaeological department. If it is likely that the artefact could be damaged or taken by someone else by leaving it, then, before removing it, mark and record the location as above and then report the matter to the local landowner; if you cannot determine who this is, then the local police will take all the necessary details. As regards stone structures such as castles, walls and buildings, or memorials or cairns that have been placed there to remember the dead, these should not be damaged or marked in any way, and none of the items placed upon these monuments should be removed.

Acknowledgements

Although this book was written alone, no work as involved as this could have been realised without the help and patience of some of my closest friends and family. To Rosie, who has spooked us on more than one occasion by encountering something on the battle site that we have not seen or heard – a rabbit or perhaps some spirit lingering from a bygone age? To Sabrina, for being patient whenever we embarked upon another Sunday 'route march' and for all her assistance with the photographs. To Imogen, whose stimulating questions have aided me in my interpretation of the disposition of the troops upon the battlefields of Powick Bridge and Montgomery, and especially for her map-reading in some of the coldest February weather I have known. To Annie, for visiting each of the sites with me and for being patient beyond measure both in the field and en route to the isolated places that we have visited, while she unwillingly learned more about the infinite variety of British military history than she had ever dreamed existed. To Derek, for his assistance with the *Archaeologia Cambrensis* and his all-round support.

While travelling the mainland of Britain through the short hours of daylight when the window of opportunity for photography was particularly fine, I have encountered wisdom, assistance and fascinating snippets of information that together have made my research so much more enjoyable. It is incredible how much local knowledge is stored about the history of 'this sceptred isle', and the fact that much of that knowledge has been passed on from parent to child makes it all the more priceless. Woods do not get known as 'Dead Men's', for no reason, lanes do not get entitled 'Gore Street' for nothing, and the answers to many small but important historical interpretations are still there just waiting to be revealed. I therefore thank all the many local people I have spoken to as I have travelled the length and breadth of Britain researching this book. Turning more to the academic side, I must thank Vanessa for her insight into the battle of Killiecrankie and the kindness that she extended to Annie and myself during our visit there, and to Ben Notley of the National Trust for Scotland for his help after my return from Scotland. My thanks also to Margaret Wilson for her tour and invaluable archives that allowed me to complete my work on St Albans, and Davina Mansell for her help, also with St Albans. My work on Norwich could not have been completed without the assistance of Brian Ayers, the County Archaeologist for Norfolk, to whom I am much indebted. To the people of Lyme Regis Philpot Museum, who allowed me to take notes from the archives and exhibits there that were relevant to the great siege. My thanks also to Tom Browning for his invaluable work on Goudhurst, especially the information on William Sturt. Giles Dickson and Winston Williamson's help was very beneficial to my investigations at Donnington. My thanks to the many tourist offices that I have visited or contacted who have forwarded bundles of guides and maps allowing me to plan my accommodation and my site visits long before I arrived at the location. My thanks to the Best Western chain of hotels, who assisted by managing to accommodate my requirements for five hotels in six nights, with Rosie, as Annie and I did our whistle-stop tour of Scotland, taking in nine battlefields in six days during blizzards and howling winds. On the battles from the English Civil War, I must express considerable gratitude to Paul Meekins, Susanne Atkin and the re-enactors from the Fairfax Battalia for their patient assistance. Finally, whole-hearted appreciation to Geoff Buxton, whose photographs came to my rescue at the eleventh hour when previously well-laid plans had been unravelled.

SPECIAL THANKS

When embarking upon an exercise as involved as a historical work that covers nine centuries of warfare, there are times when an author can become thwarted. Perhaps a vital piece of information is required to complete a chapter, or a photograph of a specific event is needed but none can be located. This section is dedicated to those people and organisations that have helped the author make this book as complete and as accurate as it can be at the time of going to print, though it is true to say that no work is ever truly finished as there is always something that could be added, or something that could be removed, or some new piece of evidence that comes to light just as the work is completed.

Geoff Buxton – photographer

To Geoff Buxton for the photographs of the Jacobites and smugglers.
Email: geoff@ewok30.freeserve.co.uk
Telephone: 01159 328216

The Mercian Guard, the Albini Household, Mark and Sarah Glover, Keith Venables

These Dark Age re-enactors provide living history and authentic Saxon, Viking and Norman displays.

Authentic Dark Age weapons and equipment can be found at Thorgrim's Emporium.

Details of the above groups can be found on the website

www.mercianguard.co.uk.

Email: thorgrim@mercianguard.co.uk

Leader Sturaesman: Paul Crossley

Secretary/Treasurer/Publicity Officer: Lucy Corke

Group Training Officer: Paul Hims

To Lucy Corke for the photographs of the above groups in action.

Paul Meekins Military & History Books

Specialising in military and social history from Roman times to the Second World War. Located at Valentines, Long Marston, Stratford-upon-Avon, CV37 8RG.

Telephone or fax: 01789 722434

Email: paul@paulmeekins.co.uk

Website: www.paulmeekins.co.uk

The Fairfax Battalia – re-enactment group

The Fairfax Battalia re-creates a seventeenth-century infantry company, and aims to entertain, educate and stimulate interest in the English Civil War period. Over the years the Battalia has built up a reputation for high standards of performance and historical accuracy, and has performed at venues such as the Tower of London and English Heritage sites. Events range from large battle re-enactments to detailed drill displays and living histories, which offer a mixture of military and civilian roles, as well as television, museum and education work. Credits include Channel 4 Time Team, BBC's History File, A History of Britain and Battlefield Britain series.

For further information, please visit the website www.fairfax.org.uk or contact Paul Meekins on 01789 722434 or via paul@paulmeekins.co.uk.

To Susanne Atkin for her photographs of the Fairfax Battalia in action.

St Albans Tourist Information Centre

To Davina Mansell for providing the swiftest responses I have ever known to an email or telephoned question. My thanks too for permission to use the picture from the re-enactment of the First Battle of St Albans.

My thanks also to the friendly staff of the Tourist and Information Centre who, with just a few days to go to the deadline of the book, provided the author with several vital pieces of information. It goes to show that they can furnish people with the necessary information whether it is on major tourist destinations or on a range of local historical, geographical or simply general information about the area.

Telephone: 01727 864511
Email: tic@stalbans.gov.uk
Website: www.stalbans.gov.uk/tourism/tic.htm

Harvington Household

To Adrian Durkin for the photograph and his assistance with the chapter on Norwich. For further information concerning the Harvington Household contact the Administrator, Harvington Hall, Harvington, near Kidderminster, Worcestershire.

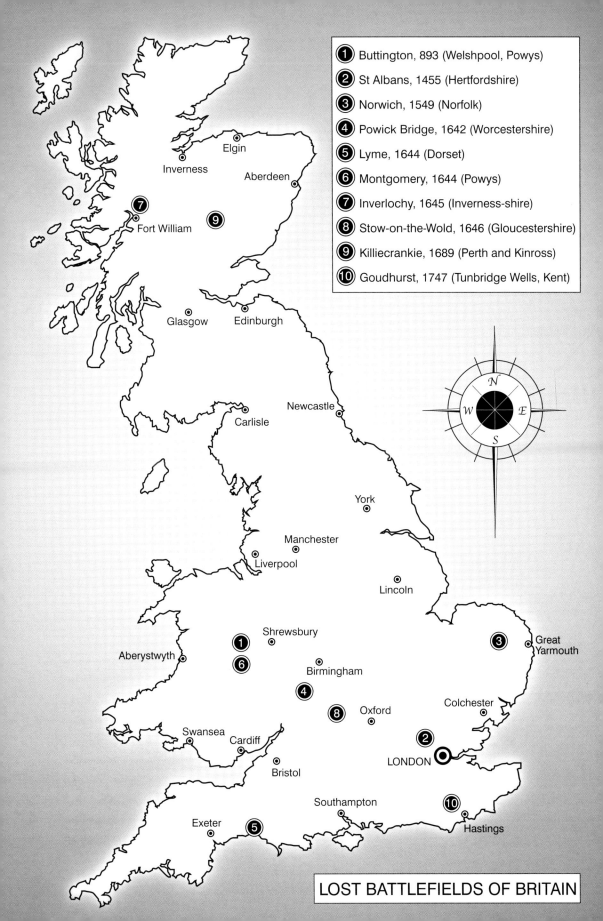

1. Buttington, 893 (Welshpool, Powys)
2. St Albans, 1455 (Hertfordshire)
3. Norwich, 1549 (Norfolk)
4. Powick Bridge, 1642 (Worcestershire)
5. Lyme, 1644 (Dorset)
6. Montgomery, 1644 (Powys)
7. Inverlochy, 1645 (Inverness-shire)
8. Stow-on-the-Wold, 1646 (Gloucestershire)
9. Killiecrankie, 1689 (Perth and Kinross)
10. Goudhurst, 1747 (Tunbridge Wells, Kent)

LOST BATTLEFIELDS OF BRITAIN

Introduction

Why lost battlefields? The famous battlefields of Hastings, Bosworth, Naseby and Culloden are etched as milestones on the journey through British history as clearly as the monoliths of Stonehenge stand upon Salisbury Plain, but these are just four battles from 2,000 years of conflict across Britain. Most books on British battlefields cover the same seventy or so battles, but if one includes the numerous sieges that have taken place at the hundreds of castles scattered across the British Isles, then England alone has at least 500 battle sites and throughout Britain there could be as many as 700, possibly even more. Importantly, each one of these battles has contributed in some way to the social, economic and political structure that we have in Britain today. The history of Britain is littered with civil war, rebellion and invasion, and over the centuries military historians have had to concentrate on, and rightly attach importance to, some battles more than others. However, in doing so they have concentrated upon no more than 100 battles. What then of the other hundreds of sites? Are the locations of these battlefields known and are any of them still visible today? What was their significance? Who were the men and women who fought and died at these 'unknown' places? My quest is to bring some of these 'lost' battlefields to light, to allow you the reader to follow in my footsteps and the footsteps of those combatants who fought long ago, little guessing at the time that they were shaping the Britain that we know today.

I have not walked these battlefields alone. When one treads across a sodden, undulating field for the first time, knowing that it is a place of conflict where men, and women, fought and died, it is sometimes important not to be alone. One needs to share the experience with other people, to understand their thoughts as they pass across the land and perhaps touch an edifice that is still standing from the time of conflict. It is helpful to be able to discuss where the troops may have advanced, stood, retreated or fallen. Accordingly I have trodden these 'lost' battlefields with my partner, Annie, our ever-faithful dog, Rosie, my youngest daughter, Imogen, and on occasion my eldest daughter, Sabrina. Together we have uncovered remarkably preserved sites, unchanged from when they were fought over, hundreds of years ago. We have found that in some areas the names of leaders involved in the conflict are used to name the parks and the streets of their local town or city. Sadly, some battlefields have been lost to the mighty earth excavators of our modern age, changing the format of the landscape forever and covering the ground with concrete-rich housing estates, reservoirs and tarmacadam roads. Other sites have been lost to more-natural attack and have been eroded by wind, rain and tide to disappear forever into the sea. In some instances it is the significance of the battle that has been lost: it may to modern historians seem of little importance, but perhaps hindsight is a distracting eye and one needs to consider those people who fought in the battle and examine the outcome in the context of its own time period. On some battlefields there are monuments erected by local people or by a national society; on others there is nothing save the vegetation that has grown and fed cattle and sheep as they have chomped their way through the grass, century after century, leaving the ground and its secrets undisturbed.

And does it matter, the issue of these battlefields that were fought over by people who perished ten, twenty or even fifty generations ago? The answer is yes, it does matter today, because even though more than 250 years have elapsed since the last of the Jacobite Rebellions, descendants of those who died still lay wreaths on the battle sites in memory of their ancestors. Yet in some cases, within twenty-four hours of those wreaths being laid, they are uplifted from their cairn, torn apart and the flowers scattered across the battlefield to rot, just as the dead would have lain centuries before. Clearly, feelings still run high and this kind of wanton, cowardly desecration merely symbolises the lack of understanding and unforgiving bigotry that runs through mankind. If we do not comprehend the past, then there can be no hope going forward. That is why these battlefields matter: people should recognise the past, understand why the battles were fought, and they should certainly carry respect for those who lost their lives; but that respect should be for the dead of both sides and not just one or the other. I carry no banner in any of these battles for any particular side; I would simply wish that after 250 years there could at least be respect for the dead.

1

Buttington – 893

WELSHPOOL, POWYS – *OS Landranger 126, Shrewsbury and Oswestry (250 090)*

Buttington is a small hamlet situated in the wide plain of the Severn valley, some four miles inside the current Welsh border, and lies close to the modern course of the River Severn. The market town of Welshpool is a further mile to the west, and the important Dark Age monument Offa's Dyke runs close by. With regard to the majority of Dark Age battle sites, modern historians have little or no written evidence to enable them to identify one location from another. This, when coupled with the lack of archaeological evidence available for those battles fought more than a thousand years ago, makes an exact identification of a battle site even harder. Given the literary and archaeological evidence available, by cross-referencing the entry for 893 in the Anglo-Saxon Chronicle with the archaeological evidence from the *Archaeologia Cambrensis*, it is clear that this hamlet of Buttington is the exact site of a long-lost Dark Age battle and, as such, Buttington is a gem among Dark Age battlefields.

PRELUDE TO BATTLE

In 893, King Alfred the Great, ruler of Wessex, was preoccupied with a Danish invasion in the south-west of England. This is supported by evidence elsewhere in the most important written source for this period, the Anglo-Saxon Chronicle. The entry for 893 states that two Danish fleets, with a combined force of 140 ships, were making for Exeter. At this time another Danish force, apparently made up from four different armies, was making its way up the River Thames and then up the River Severn, until it was overtaken by English and Welsh forces at Buttington, near Welshpool. Accordingly, King Alfred sent three ealdormen to gather what men they could to tackle this new threat, which had appeared surprisingly far inland. 'Ealdorman' was an appointed and sometimes hereditary title carried by a man who, in conjunction with the

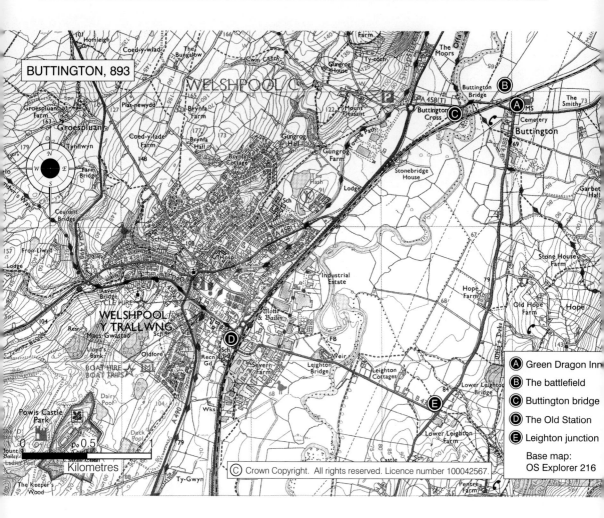

BUTTINGTON, 893

A Green Dragon Inn
B The battlefield
C Buttington bridge
D The Old Station
E Leighton junction

Base map:
OS Explorer 216

sheriff, was responsible for the administration of a shire. Their importance in military terms is that they were also responsible for commanding the armed force of their shire and leading it on behalf of the King, whenever and to wherever he commanded.

At Buttington, the Danes either occupied an existing fort or constructed a defensive position of their own. An English army on the east bank of the Severn, and a Welsh force on the west bank, had by then besieged the Danes for some weeks. This was an impossible position for the Danes because they had no way of escape without conflict and little chance that their supplies could be replenished by a relief force. Accordingly, with their food supplies gone and their numbers and fitness declining, they were left with no alternative but to try and fight their way out. To head west would be suicidal:

Looking from the Welsh side of the River Severn towards the mound on which Buttington Church stands, with the schoolroom at the centre of the picture.

they would have needed to cross the Severn and fight a Welsh army that had the advantage of ground, and with an English army at their heels. The only logical way was therefore east and back down the Severn valley, but straight into the arms of the waiting English troops. This meant that the Danes would have been facing only one enemy, as the Welsh army would probably have been forced to remain isolated on the far bank of the Severn. It seems unlikely that there was any means of crossing the Severn quickly, otherwise the Welsh would have done so earlier and defended their crossing-point against any Danish attempt to go that way.

RECONSTRUCTING THE BATTLE

It is the author's belief that at least part, if not all, of this Danish army made its way to Buttington by water. The Danes, in common with other Vikings, were master boat builders and built a variety of differently sized ships pursuant to their requirements. Modern archaeologists have proved that the Vikings successfully traded between Scandinavia, Byzantium and Russia. They achieved this by using the major rivers of eastern Europe and by rolling the ships across the land between these trading rivers, effectively making their boats into land vehicles.

All Danish ships were of shallow draught and capable of moving fast, even when rowed against wind and tide, while carrying not only men but also horses and supplies. These vessels were capable of transporting anything from a dozen to a hundred men, and on some of the ships they would work in shifts, half of the crew resting while the others rowed; this meant that the ships could be kept moving at all times. When they returned downriver, the waterway would carry them and their booty, meaning that the majority of the crew could rest before their return home, whether that was a base on the British mainland or a distant fjord in Scandinavia.

The Severn is known to have been navigable as far as Poolquay, just two miles north-east of Welshpool, until the last century. Wroxeter, located five miles west of modern Shrewsbury, was the key Roman town in Shropshire; in the second century AD it was serviced by Roman craft making their way up the Severn. Indeed the stones from which the church at Wroxeter is constructed carry marks indicating that they were once part of the Roman quay that served the 200-acre site of the city of Wroxeter.

One can imagine the scene. The Danes have rowed against the flow of the river for several days, perhaps raiding or resting up at night depending on the lands through which they were passing. Then they come to a wide-open valley with hills far away on either side. Unknown to them, the rain on the Welsh mountains has swollen the two rivers that meet west of Shrewsbury, the Vyrnwy and the Severn, causing them to burst their banks and flood the valley. The Severn would be the weaker of the two currents at this point and also the wider valley. Noting this fact, the Danes push on, unaware that the course they are now taking is across flooded marshes and not a normal riverbed.

As evening approaches they espy an old earthwork perhaps part of the great Dyke, which has been on their east side for the last few miles. They gather their boats together and use the mound as a base for the night. The Danish warriors are alerted in the night by those on watch, who have seen torches about a mile to the west on the other side of the river. Alarmingly, further torches are seen a little later on, but this time they are on the eastern side of the river from the direction of the hills that the Danes passed earlier in the day. The Danish camp stirs into life, and as dawn begins to break, those on watch are horrified to see that the river has overnight retreated some twenty yards to the west, and it is still visibly falling. The Danish ships, which had been half in and half out of the water, are now resting in tall, sodden reeds and grasses.

With full light, the harsh reality of their situation is brought home to the Danes. Their ships are stuck on sodden ground some distance from the river,

The Severn valley at Welshpool seen from the top of the Breidden Hills, showing the extent of spring flooding.

a distance that will increase unless more rains come and the river rises again. There is a Welsh army standing on the west bank of the river. Although the Welsh are out of missile range at the moment, if the Danes try and drag their ships to the river they will have to do so in the face of prolonged attack from the arrows, slings and javelins of the Welshmen. Meanwhile, to the east an English army is forming up on the lower slopes of the long mountain ridge behind them. The Danes are surrounded, a long way from their homes and a lifetime away from assistance.

At this point the Danish leaders must have held a meeting to discuss their options. Do they defend their position while they wait for the river to rise again, and so escape between both armies without having to fight? Or do they risk an all-out attack before more English and Welsh troops arrive? The Anglo-Saxon Chronicle states that they were 'encamped for many weeks', so one can safely assume that the Danes decide to consolidate their force, perhaps rationalising the ships into the minimum number required to get home, and breaking up some of the others. This will provide them with the materials to construct a rudimentary palisade around their camp as well as providing fuel for fires to cook and light their camp by night. As is the way with Britain, the rain does

DARK AGES WARFARE

Battles in this period of history were fought at very close quarters: it was not only the whites of the eyes but the spots, the sweat and the fervour that you saw on your enemy's face just before your weapons clashed together. This was warfare where death was dealt close up, with perhaps no more than 5 per cent of the casualties being caused by missile fire.

An example of a Dark Age shield-wall provided by various re-enactment groups. *(Lucy Corke, Mercian Guard re-enactment group)*

An English army of the period would have consisted largely of troops armed with a spear and a shield. Such troops could comprise as much as 80 per cent of the total force, and of these probably only one in four would have a hauberk of chain-mail to wear. Nobles would make up a further 10 per cent of the army: they would be armed with superior-quality mail and a large two-handed axe. Leaders would be similarly armed to the nobles but would have the highest-quality weapons and armour available, and would probably be the only men in the army with helmets. Both leaders and nobles took their positions in the front of the line, looking to engage their opposite number in single combat, if possible amid the confusion of battle. The lesser-armed troops, known as the 'select fyrd', would take up their positions in the second and subsequent ranks behind their better-armed superiors. The remaining 10 per cent of the force would be missile troops and skirmishers: these lightly armed troops' role was to harry and weaken the opposition by concentrating their missiles at a particular point.

The tactics for all armies at this time centred on the creation of a shield-wall with which to assault their enemies. This was a solid mass of men who interlocked shields with the men on each side before fixing their spears at the attack position. Their opponents would be similarly formed, and both sides would chant and shout insults at each other, each force trying to boost their own morale and at the same time weaken that of their opponents. Eventually the two sides would charge towards each other and a huge maul would occur as each side tried to hack and stab their enemy down by sheer brute force. The light troops would try to exploit any gap or weakness that appeared in the enemy lines. If any light troops were caught between the two opposing shield-walls as they closed together, then unless they were able to extricate themselves, either by leaping over or passing round the lines of tightly packed shields, they would simply be caught and crushed in the fight.

not fall to order and now, though the Vikings probably pray to their gods every day, no rain falls in sufficient quantity to raise the river level.

As time goes on and some warriors die from disease, hunger or wounds suffered in earlier battles, the Danes continue to rationalise their resources. This is a desperate time for them, trapped and incapable of doing anything save watching the sky for rain, sharpening their weapons for the fight that must surely come if the rains do not, with their belts getting tighter and their bodies weaker as food supplies dwindle.

Eventually the situation becomes so desperate that the Danes decide that they have to try and break out. By now, the weather has probably got much warmer, drying out the land around their remaining boats and indicating that summer is near at hand and that the likelihood of any more heavy rains has passed until the autumn. Almost all of their food is gone, but the Danes need strength to fight their way out. Their only source of fresh food is their horses, so in desperation they kill sufficient of them to feed the remaining men; perhaps, as only one horse head was found in the burial pits, one horse was sufficient to feed the whole force. They plan to break out in the last light of evening, after they have rested all day; this will give them a chance to run through the English lines and then scatter into the darkness of night, in an 'every man for himself' situation. Accordingly they have one last meal together, calling one last time on their gods to assist them before they prepare for battle.

Faced with only one course of action the Danes break out of their encampment and assault the English lines. Danish armies only ever contained a few horsemen; perhaps these lead the charge to try and punch a hole through the English lines, followed by the bulk of the Danish force. Perhaps some Danes try dragging a number of the smallest boats to the river to attempt and escape by that route, while the rest of the army holds the English host at bay. The darkness helps to protect the Danes if they advance towards the Welsh army, who undoubtedly watch the battle unfold before them across the valley.

The fighting is evidently fierce as a named king's thegn, Ordheah, is killed, along with many other English thegns. At this time, a thegn was a landowner with an income of more than four hides per year, whereas to become a king's thegn meant that the landowner had an income of more than forty hides per year. There is still much debate as to what area a hide covered. A hide is defined as the land necessary to keep one family for a year, and varies on interpretation between 30 and 120 acres. Some of the Danes escape – perhaps those few that had horses left to carry them – but clearly the battle is won by 'the Christians' (the English) and there is 'a very great slaughter of the Danes' (*The Anglo-Saxon Chronicle*, tr. Dorothy Whitelock, Eyre and Spottiswode, 1961, p. 56). Eventually, when there are no Danes left fighting, their opponents collect their bodies and take the Danes' weapons, armour and anything of value. Perhaps the English have mounted troops who undertake some kind of pursuit to try and hunt down those few Danes who have succeeded in escaping.

This brings an important question and the most difficult one to answer: that of the numbers involved in this battle. We know from the *Archaeologia Cambrensis* that exactly 400 skulls and associated bones were found in the three burial pits discovered under the churchyard, but were all of these Danish dead? We know from the Anglo-Saxon Chronicle that some Danes escaped 'by flight', but the word 'slaughter' suggests that the majority of the Danes were killed. With this in mind it seems likely that the Danish army was no more than 500 strong, which would make the size of the fleet between ten and fifteen ships depending on their capacity.

The action of the Danes can also provide a clue as to the size of the English army. The Danes adopted a defensive position, which would suggest that their

Buttington Church. The burial pits lay underneath the schoolroom, which is at the far end of the churchyard. The ancient yew tree is said to have been planted to commemorate the battle.

army was significantly smaller than the English. Had the Danish force been anywhere near equal in size to the English then they would have attacked at once, rather than risking the arrival of more English troops and by so doing giving the English the advantage in numbers.

At first glance, the Welsh army is even more difficult to gauge, but as it opted not to try and interfere in the battle, choosing instead to adopt a holding position on the far bank of the Severn, it would suggest that the army was smaller than the English, and therefore possibly smaller than the Danish force as well. The advantage of ground may have been sufficient for the Welsh to be sure that the Danes could progress no further west, but it is also apparent that the Welsh army was not large enough for the Danes to be worried about a direct Welsh assault on their own defensive position and stranded ships.

THE BATTLEFIELD TODAY

Despite extensive research, no one from the local secular community is able to complete the full history of All Saints Church at Buttington. Legend has it that a church was built on the mound to commemorate this victory over the Danes, but there is no evidence as yet to support this, though the yew tree has been dated to 893. The current church is believed to be of seventeenth-century construction, upon a much earlier medieval base. All Saints Church today sits upon a small mound, with a deep ditch running along its eastern edge, and roads upon its western and northern edges. These all lie below the level of the church mound and form exactly the kind of site that a force would select as a protected position. One can only speculate as to what was here before the church was built and before the Danes arrived. Given the amount of Roman and Celtic remains in the area and its close proximity to Offa's Dyke, perhaps the Danes occupied what was an already prepared, if long-abandoned, defensive earthwork.

In 1838, while digging foundations for a new schoolroom at the south-west corner of Buttington churchyard, the Revd Richard Dawkins made a remarkable discovery: he uncovered three pits. The largest contained 200 skulls, and the other two pits each contained 100 skulls. The sides of each pit were lined with human arm and leg bones. All the teeth within the skulls were perfect, suggesting that the men were in the prime of life. Some of the bones showed signs of violent death, as some of the skulls had been fractured. Horse bones and teeth were also found in the pits. All of these bones were collected and reinterred on the north side of the churchyard, save for many of the teeth, which were sold off by the workmen who were performing the reburial (it was believed at the time that a dead man's tooth was a cure for toothache, and the workmen received between 6d and 1s for each tooth – 2½ to 5 pence in our modern coinage and equivalent to around £2 today).

Revd Dawkins later wrote about his discovery in the journal *Archaeologia Cambrensis* (1873), vol. 28, pp. 214–15. Whether these burial pits were made at the time of the battle, or created subsequently when the site became consecrated, is at present unknown but in his article, Dawkins speculated that the latter is probably the more likely.

So why was the battle fought here? We know that the English pursued the Danes for between 160 and 200 miles, depending on the route taken, from the Thames all the way to the Welsh border; what we do not know is whether they marched on foot or rowed upriver. The author has lived long enough within the confines of this part of the Severn valley to see the dramatic moods that the River Severn can portray. Despite the controls of the Clywedog Dam, the river still regularly bursts its banks, causing chaos to the modern transportation system by flooding road and rail routes, sometimes causing their closure. The Severn, which is in places only a few metres wide, can flood the valley to the width of a mile after just forty-eight hours of rain. Imagine how much greater the rise and fall of the river would be in the days before the Clywedog Dam was built; in those times much of the valley would be nothing more than soft marsh land. Importantly, when the river does flood, much of the side water is sluggish, as calm as a lake. It would be perfect for craft to move upon, particularly when the land was not enclosed with hedges and walls and punctuated by scattered farm buildings, as it is today.

EXPLORING THE BATTLE SITE

The site can be explored on foot; it is a round journey just short of four miles and takes approximately two hours to perform. There are no steep slopes or tricky sections on the route, but care needs to be taken on some stretches, as they are along country roads with no pavements. The site can also be circumnavigated by car, and there is parking available along the majority of roads, so that stops can be made as required to view the different aspects of the location. For those visitors arriving by train, Welshpool is served by a main railway link running from Shrewsbury to Aberystwyth. The station is located on the edge of the town and is conveniently placed for exploring the site. The visitor need only cross the footbridge and then pick up the walk at point D, the Old Station.

The hamlet of Buttington straddles the A458 Shrewsbury to Welshpool road, and has three landmarks: a church, a public house and a level crossing. If you are approaching from Shrewsbury, the church on the left and the Green Dragon Inn on your right are the first landmarks to look out for: this is point A on the map. The church sits upon the mound that was probably used by the Danes as their defensive position. The battle itself would have taken place behind the Green Dragon Inn and across the now enclosed fields heading east towards a small range of hills, known as the Breiddens.

If you have approached Buttington from the Shrewsbury direction then you will have already travelled alongside these hills, upon which sits a large Iron Age hill fort and a monument to Admiral Rodney. Parking is possible by turning at point A west towards Leighton on the B4388, effectively opposite

An ancient oak stands in a flooded field on the most likely site for the battle of Buttington.

the Green Dragon Inn, and between the church and its current churchyard, which sits in the left-hand corner of the T-junction. Parking is allowed along this section of the road, identified by a telephone box.

It is worth leaving the car at this point and exploring the churchyard and its surrounds. At the rear of the church is an ancient yew, which is said to have been planted to commemorate the English success at the battle. The visitor will also see the schoolroom. It was the digging of the foundations for this stone building that led to the discovery of the burial pits by Revd Dawkins. The visitor will also note the height of the mound over the surrounding fields, only a few feet but sufficient to give the occupier the advantage of ground. If the Severn is in spate, it is possible that all the fields below will be underwater; if not, then the distant bridge and line of trees to the south-west indicate the current course of the river.

ANGLO-SAXON CHRONICLE

'When the King had turned west with the army towards Exeter, as I have said before, and the Danish army had laid siege to the borough, they went to their ships when he arrived there. When he [the King] was occupied against the army there in the west, and the [other] two Danish armies were assembled at Shoebury in Essex, and had made a fortress there, they went both together up along the Thames, and a great reinforcement came to them both from the East Angles and the Northumbrians. They then went up along the Thames until they reached the Severn, then up along the Severn. Then Ealdorman Ethelred and Ealdorman Aethelhelm and Ealdorman Aethelnoth and the King's thegns who then were at home at the fortresses assembled from every borough east of the Parret, and both west and east of the Selwood, and also north of the Thames and west of the Severn, and also some portion of the Welsh people. When they were all assembled, they overtook the Danish army at Buttington, on the bank of the Severn, and besieged it on every side in a fortress. Then when they had encamped for many weeks on the two sides of the river, and the King was occupied in the west in Devon against the naval force, the besieged were oppressed by famine, and had eaten the greater part of their horses and the rest had died of starvation. Then they came out against the men who were encamped on the east side of the river, and fought against them, and the Christians had the victory. And the King's thegn Ordheah and also many other King's thegns were killed and very great slaughter of the Danes was made, and the part that escaped were saved by flight.'
(*The Anglo-Saxon Chronicle*, tr. D. Whitelock, entry for year 893/4, pp. 55–6)

Continuing on foot, the visitor should walk toward the river along the A458 with the church now behind, and, once past the level crossing, cross the road and look back east behind the Green Dragon Inn. According to the Anglo-Saxon Chronicle, it would seem that the lowland before you is where the battle took place. You are now at point B on the map.

Continue a little further on towards Welshpool, to where the road sweeps to the left in order to cross the River Severn, point C on the map. Swing right, then continue ahead to meet the A483, the main road from Oswestry, Wrexham and Chester to the north, at a traffic island. Stand on the bridge and look back towards the church, somewhat obscured by the modern railway bridge: this is the view that the Welsh forces would have had as they stood and waited for the Danes to decide upon their course of action.

Turn left at this island and continue along the A483 towards Welshpool. After two miles you will see a modern railway station on your left and a railway station building ahead of you, on opposite sides of the main road. The latter is the Old Station and marked on the map as point D. This listed building is now a large country clothing store with refreshments and conveniences on site. Note that this is an excellent place to leave your vehicle if you are planning to traverse the whole route on foot.

To continue your circumnavigation it is necessary to take the road that turns left out of the Old Station and proceed over a large bridge that spans both road and railway. You are now on a feeder road for the industrial area of Welshpool. At the next traffic island turn right and proceed along the B4381, which is a fairly straight road leading to Leighton. This road crosses the River Severn just after leaving the town boundary, and arrives at Leighton at a T-junction on the B4388, point E on the map. Turn left and return along the B4388 to come back to point A at Buttington. This part of the route runs along the foot of Long Mountain and provides an excellent view back to Welshpool across the Severn valley.

As an alternative to walking along the A483 main road from points C to D, it is possible to walk along the towpath of the Shropshire Union Canal, clearly marked on the map. This walk brings the visitor out into Welshpool halfway between the town centre and the Old Station, and turning down the road will bring the visitor back to the Old Station.

CONCLUSIONS

Buttington is a significant battle because, when all the evidence is put together, the location can be pinpointed. It is also one of those rare occasions in the history of the Viking incursions when the English slaughtered their Danish opponents. Much has been made of the defensive tactics developed by Alfred the Great in the 880s. According to David Smurthwaite in his book, *The Complete Guide to the Battlefields of Britain*, it was these tactics that enabled him to force the Vikings either to accept Danelaw or return home in the year 896. Buttington is not mentioned in Smurthwaite's book; but surely if 896 was the key year for the Vikings to admit that they had had enough of war, then the news of the battle of Buttington in 893, filtering over time through to the Viking leaders, must have played a significant part in influencing them. The Vikings realised that they could not afford to sustain a war against the English if they were going to suffer such complete defeats as they had done on the upper reaches of the River Severn. The Dark Ages span over 600 years of European history and they are called 'Dark' simply because there is a lack of written and archaeological evidence to clarify what took place in those turbulent years between 409 and 1066. To the historian, therefore, Buttington is a most valuable site, because here the main written source for this period, the Anglo-Saxon Chronicle, is supported by the discovery of the hundreds of bodies that were systematically buried so close to the battle site.

LOCAL ATTRACTIONS

Welshpool is a busy market town, and boasts a high street with many common names above the door. There are a number of hotels and guesthouses scattered around the town, and plenty of cafés, tearooms and public houses. Monday is market day, when the town is vibrant with one of the largest livestock markets in the United Kingdom. The nearest railway station is to be found opposite the Old Station, which is point D on the map. The tourist information centre is located at Vicarage Gardens, Welshpool; telephone 01938 552043.

Powis Castle and Garden, Welshpool, Powys. [Telephone: 01938 551929. Website: www.nationaltrust.org.uk. The castle and gardens are not open all the year round; contact the castle before visiting. There is an admission charge.] The castle and its spectacular gardens are maintained by the National Trust, and are located just one mile south-west from Welshpool town centre and can be reached by taking the A490 Newtown road from Welshpool town centre and following the appropriate signs. There is ample parking at Powis Castle. However, there is also a public footpath that leads from the left-hand side of Welshpool high street and can be found at the bottom of a pay car park, just above the Town Hall, which is on the opposite, right-hand side. The path meanders through the grounds of the estate in which herds of deer and cattle graze, before reaching the castle. Importantly, this footpath is open all the year round, allowing the visitor arriving out of season to see this impressive 900-year-old castle from the outside. The castle itself houses a remarkable collection of artefacts that belonged to Clive of India, as well as impressive fine art and furniture.

The Welshpool and Llanfair Caereinion Light Railway. [Telephone: 01938 810441. No website. The railway is not open all the year round but they do run special trips out of season so it is best to contact the organisation before visiting. There is no admission charge to the site, but fares have to be paid to travel on the trains.] The line runs from the station at Welshpool through some picturesque hills and river valleys for a distance of eleven miles to the village of Llanfair Caereinion. The station is reached by following Welshpool high street to the top and then continuing on the same road until the Raven public house appears on the left. The entrance to the railway site and the visitors' car parks is on the left-hand side of the traffic island now ahead of you.

Powysland Museum, Welshpool, Powys. [Telephone: 01938 554656. No website. There are specific opening times, so contact the centre before visiting. There is no admission charge.] The museum is located in Severn Street, which runs from the Old Station to the high street, alongside the canal. The museum contains details on local history, from the earliest prehistoric settlers to Montgomeryshire people in the last century. There is also information on the railway and canal systems that helped to shape the county.

2

St Albans – 22 May 1455

HERTFORDSHIRE – *OS Landranger 166, Luton and Hertford, Hitchin and St Albans (147 071)*

St Albans is one of the few cities in Britain where hand-to-hand fighting between large bodies of men took place in the streets, but the very fact that the battle was fought within the confines of a city has led to its exclusion from some leading books on British battlefields. St Albans is a crucial event in British history because it was the first battle of the Wars of the Roses and it would spark a series of conflicts that would last for thirty-two years. Once the talking was done and war was inevitable, the location of the small settlement of St Albans, lying close to the Great North Road, was a strategically important place for those armies marching to or from London. St Albans would see a battle unlike any before in British history and its like has rarely been seen since. It would make the reputation of the young Richard Neville, Earl of Warwick: he was just 25 at the time, but following his success at St Albans he would go on to become known as Warwick 'the Kingmaker'.

PRELUDE TO BATTLE

The chaotic and inconsistent government that Henry VI had practised directly led to the armed rebellion that Richard of York now led against him. Henry VI, having learned that certain members of the court had fled London, held council with those closest to him and decided that the only way to resolve the issues that now beset the kingdom was by holding a great council, a parliament in effect, at which the grievances of all the nobles could be heard. Accordingly, writs were sent out on 21 April 1455, summoning all the nobles of the land to meet on 21 May at Leicester. Richard of York, who had been arrested at the previous parley, decided that his attendance would only result in his downfall and, together with the Earl of Warwick and the Earl of Salisbury, he marched

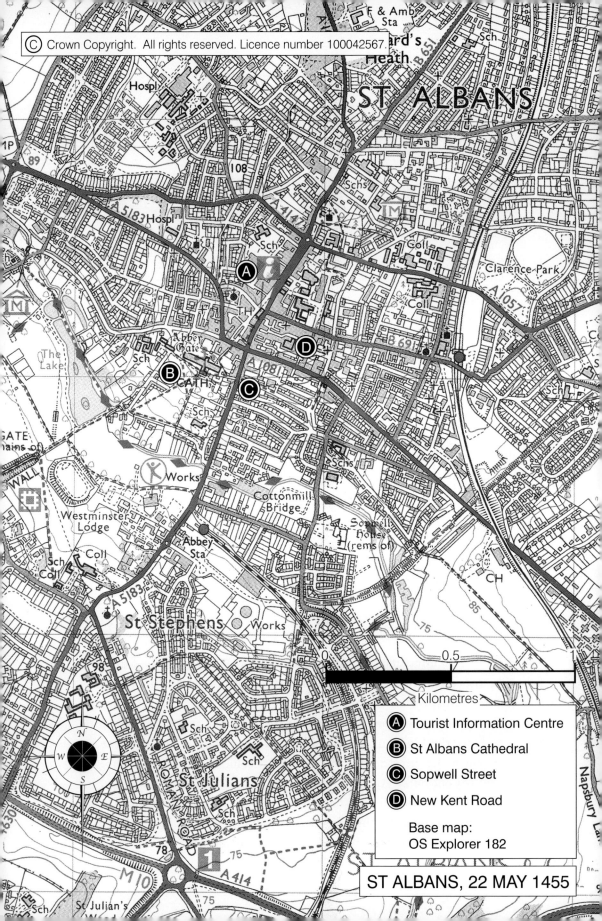

ST ALBANS

(A) Tourist Information Centre

(B) St Albans Cathedral

(C) Sopwell Street

(D) New Kent Road

Base map:
OS Explorer 182

ST ALBANS, 22 MAY 1455

with 3,000 men towards London. York's plan was to intercept the King as he marched north towards Leicester and take Henry VI under his protection and away from the clutches of the Duke of Somerset and his allies. York's loyalty to the King is shown by the fact that while en route to St Albans he twice wrote letters informing Henry that their argument was with Somerset and not the King, and that if Somerset was removed then the Yorkist forces would disperse. Henry's inconsistency in his approach to government is demonstrated by the fact that on the eve of battle he replaced the commander-in-chief of his army, Somerset, with Buckingham, a relation of York's, but still retained Somerset as a counsellor. Despite all of the correspondence between the factions, both armies arrived at St Albans early on the morning of 22 May. The King and the Lancastrian forces were arrayed in the centre of the city and took up defensive positions at the gates that blocked each route into the centre. The city was surrounded by a dry ditch upon which, on the city side, was a wooden palisade. The Yorkist army was on the east side of the city and centred on the butts, fields set aside for the militia to practise their archery and drill.

Having deployed their armies, the leaders of both sides in time-honoured tradition met to discuss the situation and to see whether bloodshed could be avoided. The King refused to discharge Somerset and York refused to disband his army until Somerset was surrendered. It was an impasse: the parley was over and the battle began as soon as York returned to his men.

RECONSTRUCTING THE BATTLE

The course of the battle is not difficult to piece together, since the Abbot of St Albans watched the battle from the cathedral tower and afterwards wrote an account of the events he saw, and accordingly there is little dispute among historians as to the course of the battle. Members of the St Albans and Hertfordshire Architectural and Archaeological Society have visited the tower and even today, despite the fact that the average height of all the buildings within the city has been raised considerably, the original street plan over which the battle unfolded is clearly visible. Extracts from the Abbot's account are reproduced in *The Battles and Battlefields of Saint Albans, 1455–1461* by Charles Ashdown, Gibbs and Bamforth, no year of publication. Sadly, the cathedral tower is not open to the general public and those few lucky enough to have visited the roof say that the journey is not for the faint-hearted or those who suffer from vertigo. To understand the battle, it is necessary to picture the terrain of the city. St Albans sits proudly atop a small ridge, and around the city then ran a

THE CAUSES OF THE WARS OF THE ROSES

Who should rule England? It may sound a simple definition but in essence the chaos and decades of brutal warfare and revenge killings that became known as the Wars of the Roses all stemmed from the fact that Henry VI was a weak and sickly king. Richard Plantagenet, Duke of York and Henry VI's third cousin once removed, was a respected man, popular among noble and commoner alike. Indeed, if Henry VI was to die without issue, then Richard was to ascend to the throne. But upon his recovery the King restored Edmund Beaufort, Duke of Somerset, to his former position of 'royal favourite'. Although Somerset was unpopular in the country, his access to the King's ear was enough to ensure that his policies were approved. No doubt at Somerset's bidding, York was 'exiled' first to the position of Lieutenant of France and then to Lieutenant of Ireland. The King then made Somerset Lieutenant of France and awarded him £25,000 to maintain the few English strongholds left there. York was incensed by this move, not least because he had forked out almost £40,000 of his own money to maintain those defences while he had held the position. Somerset's inability to command or organise led to further English losses in France, including Rouen; yet on his return to London he was still welcomed with open arms by Henry VI.

The mood of the country was deteriorating and a revolt in 1450, led by Jack Cade and supported by some of the nobility, claimed to be the voice of the common people and called for Somerset's removal. York continued to fume and returned from Ireland in September 1450. Despite attempts to apprehend him, he presented himself at court and put himself forward as a champion of law and order. Knowing that York had tremendous public support, the King backed down from his attempted apprehension of him. York now retired to his home, for the moment biding his time and waiting for the correct time to act. He deemed that the spring of 1452 was that time: as the situation in France worsened, he called his retinue together and marched on London. Unfortunately, little support came from the other nobles of England. Yet York pressed on, undaunted, and waited at Blackheath, a traditional meeting place outside London, to parley with King Henry VI. After hearing York's demands, the King agreed to arrest Somerset on the grounds of his mismanagement of his lieutenancy in France, his appalling judgement in matters of state and his continual misguided advice to the King. In accordance with the King's wishes, York disbanded his army and went to the King's tent as requested, only to find Somerset on the King's right hand and himself now under arrest. After three months in prison York swore an oath never again to take up arms against the King and was duly released with the news ringing in his ears that the Queen, Margaret of Anjou, was pregnant, and that he would now be a step lower down the ladder on any claim to the throne of

A re-enactment group in authentic Wars of the Roses costume act out the first battle of St Albans. *(Davina Mansell, Tourist Information Centre, © St Albans Festival)*

England. Having alienated the Duke of York, Henry VI now frustrated the Earl of Warwick (Richard Neville) by giving some of his lands in Wales to Somerset.

Tensions were rising in the shires as well as at court. The Percys and Nevilles had been rivals for many decades and the marriage of Thomas Neville to Maude Stanhope meant that long-lost Percy lands (confiscated following their rebellion against Henry IV at Shrewsbury in 1403) were going to end up in Neville hands. This was too much for the Percys and they began a series of raids on Neville estates, which provoked a series of counter-raids on the estates of the Percy family. The commoners of England were lamenting the loss of even more of their rich ports and cities in France and the high levels of taxation being imposed upon them to pay for the French wars, and this, coupled with the feuding that was now splitting the nobility, meant that England was in a sorry state.

Just when strong, decisive leadership was required, Henry VI had a nervous breakdown, and it looked likely that Somerset would become the protector of a people who hated him; but the Neville family, incensed by recent events, supported the Duke of York, and Richard Plantagenet was appointed to rule England as protector. Somerset, for all his scheming, found himself locked in the Tower under a charge of treason for his French debacle, but the country was destined to be rocked again when, in January 1455, Henry VI suddenly became well again and released Somerset back into society. The Percys, fearing for their safety while York had been protector, now found an ally in Somerset and they offered allegiance to him, trusting that they would get both Somerset and the King's support against the Nevilles. This created an alliance between the Nevilles and York, who left London with the aim of gathering their forces, because they knew that from now on they would have to back their beliefs with force. The Wars of the Roses, which commenced with just six main families involved, would spread like the virulent plagues of the time across the whole of the realm, enveloping all the main noble families of the day, resulting in their death and destruction, and weakening Britain's position as a power in Europe for the next hundred years.

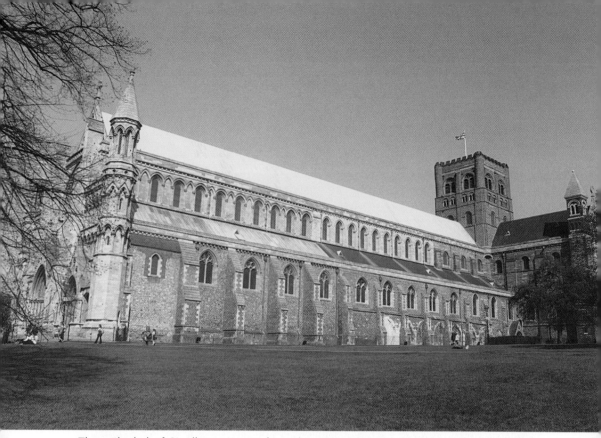

The cathedral of St Albans. It was from this tower that the Abbot watched the battle below him.

defensive dry ditch, which was known as 'Ton Man Ditch'. On the city side of this ditch was a wooden palisade as a further means of defence. All of the routes into the city crossed this ditch at right angles by means of a small bridge, after which the lane or track would pass between houses and shops before arriving at the defensive gate for that particular street, quite close to the city centre.

When the 3,000-strong Yorkist army deployed on the east side of the ditch, Buckingham positioned the King's army, which numbered a mere 2,000, to defend the gates on the eastern routes into the town. He also placed a reserve to be close to the central market square, so that they could reinforce any weak points identified once the battle began. Buckingham ensured that all the gates were barricaded to reinforce his defences against a fairly predictable line of attack; after all there were no other ways in. Buckingham's plan was a sound defensive strategy: he had 1,000 fewer men than the Yorkists, but he had a city to defend, there was not a lot of room for fighting and access for the attackers would be up the narrow confines of the eastern lanes. With the initial parley soon over, York returned to his men and at once an attack was launched upon the gates across Shropshire Lane (now Victoria Street) and Sopwell Lane, at least

The Cheltenham and Gloucester Building Society marks the spot where Warwick smashed through the house to attack the Lancastrian rear.

part of which was known as London Road at the time of the battle. Initially the Yorkist attack looked as though it would succeed: the element of surprise was with them and they almost carried the day. However, seeing the initial Yorkist attack, Buckingham threw some of his reserves behind the gates to strengthen their defences. This worked, because the Yorkists began to take heavy casualties.

At the back of all the houses around the city, long, thin gardens ran all the way down to the ditch. Warwick, who was fortunate enough to see this, realised that there could be a way into the city other than through the gates. Picking a spot between the two gates where the fighting was still continuing, Warwick led some of his archers, and possibly his mercenary Burgundian handgunners, through the gardens along what is now New Kent Road. Then, once he had succeeded in getting all of his men to the rear of the houses, they hacked their way through the walls, which presumably would have been timber-frame wattle and daub structures, and broke out into Holywell Street, before charging into the market square with cries of 'a Warwick, a Warwick'. Faced by an enemy pouring on them from the rear the King's army capitulated. The reserve in the market place, who were protecting the King and his nobles, were shot at by the archers at very close range and numerous members of the nobility, including the King, were wounded. The Abbot vividly describes the severing of limbs and heads as the battle raged below him, 'the whole street full of bodies, lying here, there and everywhere' (Ashdown, *Battles and Battlefields*, p. 10). How many were killed in the battle is another matter for speculation, but it seems, taking the average from a range of sources, that 800 to 1,000 dead is the likeliest figure, of which probably at least a quarter were Yorkists killed in their attempted assaults on the gates. What is known is that sixty-seven members of the noble aristocracy took part in the battle, and that eleven were killed and four wounded and captured, which amounts to half of the thirty Lancastrian nobility present. None of the thirty-seven Yorkist nobles were killed or captured, confirming what an overwhelming victory this was for Richard of York and his cause. The majority of the Lancastrians surrendered but Somerset, clearly knowing that his day was done, chose to fight to the end, dying in the street on the corner of Shropshire Lane and the market square. Somerset was fourth in line to the throne on the Lancastrian side and the first potential 'heir' to die in the war, but he would turn out to be first of many. Interestingly, a fortune-teller had told Somerset that he would die in the shadow of a castle. Accordingly the King had sympathised with Somerset's wishes and not invited him to court at Windsor. How strange then are the turns of fate, for when Somerset was slain he fell outside the Castle Inn.

The plaque on the wall of the Skipton Building Society in Victoria Street commemorates where Somerset, the instigator of the conflict, died.

THE BATTLEFIELD TODAY

The problem for the modern historian in St Albans is that shopping centres, car parks and houses have been built upon and now cover all the traces of the original city; only when demolition and rebuilding occurs can any archaeological fieldwork be done. This is what has deterred some historians from including the battle of St Albans in their books, which is a pity because there is still much to appreciate despite the lack of original ground to walk on. Sadly, however, the majority of buildings that lined the streets in the fifteenth century have been lost, to be replaced by an array of Victorian and modern shops and offices, but the street pattern that existed in 1455 can still be discerned. The course of the defensive Ton Man Ditch now lies beneath Marlborough Road and Keyfield Terrace. At right angles to this ditch were the two lanes that led into the city: Shropshire Lane – now known as Victoria Street – and what was Old London Road/Sopwell Lane – today just Sopwell Lane. This must not be confused with London Road, which has been built since the battle of St Albans to the north of the original London (hence Old London) Road. These two roads, Victoria Street and Sopwell Lane, are the routes into the city which the Yorkist forces initially attacked. Immediately south of and parallel to Victoria Street is a small road leading to the rear of a multi-storey car park and shopping centre. This is New Kent Road, and marks the route which Warwick took across the gardens there at the time, before breaking through the house and charging into the square beyond. Fortunately, the market place is still in the same location as it was when the battle was fought.

EXPLORING THE BATTLE SITE

St Albans is a battle to be explored on foot, and as the whole route, including taking in the cathedral, is only a little over a mile, it is a most rewarding and compact site to explore. As in any city, car parking can be an issue, but there are numerous car parks around the city, so one should never be too far from the centre. The most convenient and certainly a reasonably priced car park is that of the Maltings, which could not be more convenient for the person exploring the battle, as the entrance lies in Victoria Street. Once the vehicle has been safely stowed, make for the tourist information centre, which is in the market place in the centre of the city; this is point A on the map. If you do not have a map of the city, then it is worth obtaining one from the tourist information centre before setting out on your walk. From here, walk south down Market Street until you

ARMIES IN THE WARS OF THE ROSES

A typical army of this period was led by a prominent member of the nobility, often one of the York or Lancastrian heirs to the throne, and these figureheads would be supported by lesser nobility loyal to one house or the other. The bulk of the army would be made up of the retinues (paid professional soldiers and servants) from these noble families; the wealthier the noble and the larger his estates, the bigger the army would be. If a noble did not have his own army, he might well hire foreign mercenaries to bolster his military importance. The core of both the Yorkist and Lancastrian armies therefore was virtually the same; the differences came according to the different types of local militias and mercenaries that fought alongside the leading nobles and their retinues. The foreign mercenaries who were hired in increasing numbers as the Wars of the Roses wore on were normally handgunners and crossbowmen from Germany, Burgundy and France, and pikemen from Germany. As with all 'English' civil wars, troops fought and died from Ireland, Wales and Scotland alongside their English cousins. These 'Celtic' warriors were often light spearmen, archers, axemen and javelinmen, poorly armed and in hierarchy the lowest of the low on the battlefield. Women could also be present among the nobility: Margaret of Anjou personally led the Lancastrians after the capture of King Henry VI at Northampton in 1460 and proved herself to be a most able commander and strategist.

The nobility who led the army and their men-at-arms would make up no more than 5 per cent of the total force. These 'knights' would be fully armoured and a few would ride armoured horses during battle, accompanied by their standard bearers, pages, squires and other attendants. The majority of these men-at-arms, however, even though they were fully armoured as if they were mounted knights, chose to dismount and fight on foot, choosing either the long spear or more commonly the halberd as their principal weapon.

After the 'professional' trained soldier would come the mainstay of the army, the bowmen. On average, at least 60 per cent of the force would be archers, trained men who practised regularly, drawn from either the retinue of nobles or levied from the shire in which they lived. These men had gained a fearful reputation when fighting the French over the last fifty years and their showers of arrows were the most potent weapon of the day. The next 15 per cent of the army would be heavy infantry, armoured men who fought with the bill, halberd or other polearm, shaped like a 'can-opener' and designed for ripping apart the heavy armour that their opponents, especially the men-at-arms and nobility, now wore for protection.

All of these troops detailed above would wear some kind of livery to tell themselves apart on the field of battle. These were the 'football' colours of the day and would normally reflect in their design the colours upon the coat of arms of the noble who employed them. In addition, a password and field device would be given to the army before battle commenced to allow each side to distinguish itself from the other. The password would be a simple name or phrase; the field device could be a sprig of holly, oak or some other abundant vegetation that could be fixed into a belt or hat.

The remaining 20 per cent of the army would be made up from a variety of troop types, though their numbers varied according to the nobles involved and the geographical location of the battle. There would be groups of mercenaries as detailed above, and units of light 'Celtic' troops that were used to bolster the rear ranks of the better-armoured foot or to hold rough areas of terrain, such as woods, from being occupied by the enemy. There might also be small groups of light horsemen, 'currours', whose role was to scout, take messages and protect the flanks of the large infantry battalions once deployed on the battlefield.

The final part of an army, and one which was slowly growing in importance, was the artillery. Cannon in the fifteenth century were as varied as the colours that the troops wore and their reliability was as questionable as the nobles who hired them. Many cannon barrels simply sat in wooden boxes or frames and once deployed were difficult to manoeuvre. The rough powder of the time made their effectiveness inconsistent. However, their gradual introduction had a certain novelty factor and no army of the period would now consider itself complete unless it had some 'ordnance' with which to harass the enemy.

come to the High Street, with the old clock tower looming above you. Turn right and then follow the road down to the cathedral, point B on the map. The tower of this impressive medieval building is the spot from where the Abbot watched the battle and, following the battle, where some of the dead Lancastrian nobles were buried. After exploring the cathedral, return up the High Street and turn right at the lights, proceeding down Holywell Hill. After a few hundred yards there is a left turn into Sopwell Street, with a fine half-timbered building on the right-hand side, point C on the map. This is the first of the two gated routes into the city through which the Yorkist forces tried to enter. One can imagine how deadly the archery from the defenders would be in such a confined space: every arrow would make a mark. Proceed down Sopwell Lane until there is a left turn into Keyfield Terrace. You have now turned to walk on the road that marks where Ton Man Ditch originally ran. Follow this road to the crossroads with London Road, but remember that this London Road did not exist in 1455. Proceed now into Marlborough Road, still on the route of Ton Man Ditch.

Annie with Rosie and Margaret Wilson survey New Kent Road, the location of the gardens that Warwick crossed to bypass the gates of the city.

The next road on the left, point D on the map, is New Kent Road, and this is where Warwick led his surprise attack through the gardens of the houses, out on to what is now Chequer Street and, at the time of print, the Cheltenham and Gloucester Building Society. Continue past New Kent Road, halting at the next crossroads, which is where Shropshire Lane (now Victoria Street) met Ton Man Ditch. To the right and lower end of Shropshire Lane, which was also known as Long Butts Lane, is where the butts field would have been, the sports field of medieval England where the longbowmen and militia would have practised their skills. Interestingly, the monarchy was so concerned about the spread of a game called 'football', which the people were preferring to play rather than practise their archery, that Edward III, Richard II and Henry IV all attempted to ban it. From this crossroads, turn east and head up modern Victoria Street, passing the entrance to the car park on the left. This was the second gated route into the city, through which Warwick originally attempted to gain entry. At the very top of the road on the right-hand side is a plaque commemorating the death of the Duke of Somerset, the Castle Inn which was there at the time of the battle being long since gone. Just over the road is the tourist information centre, back at point A on the map.

CONCLUSIONS

St Albans was yet another turning point on the meandering course that is the history of this nation. The weak, inept and inconsistent Henry VI had created a situation which only military action could solve. York went on to provide stable government for some months after his victory at St Albans while the King was sickly again, but all too quickly Henry returned to the throne and the scheming and plotting resumed. The scourge of war followed soon after. St Albans was the start of thirty-two years of warfare, still remembered today when Lancashire play Yorkshire at cricket in the 'Roses' matches. It is a pity that such pretty red and white flowers should be the badges of these warring houses that were responsible for the deaths of tens of thousands of men and many tens of nobles during these bitter wars. St Albans was also responsible for making the name of the Earl of Warwick, whose own scheming and eventual change of sides would result in his losing his own head. Warwick, though, deserves to be remembered for other events at the battle of St Albans. Whether or not it was solely his idea to hack through the house and so gain entry to the city is not known, but Warwick takes the credit because he led the initiative that resulted in a resounding victory. Also, he used a unit of mercenary handgunners, probably the first time that a hand-held gun had been fired in Britain; it is a good thing that our savage city streets today are not attributable to the legacy of one man.

LOCAL ATTRACTIONS

St Albans is a thriving historical city, with a modern café feel to some of the streets. There are many places to stay, ranging from hotels to guesthouses and inns, and a quite superb range of restaurants which provide an enviable choice of international cuisine. The nearest railway station is in St Albans. The tourist information centre is located at the Town Hall, Market Place, St Albans; telephone 01727 864511.

Cathedral and Abbey Church of St Alban. [Telephone: 01727 860780. Website: www.stalbanscathedral.org.uk. Open all the year round. There is no admission charge.] Dedicated to St Alban, the first British martyr. A relic from the saint's body is entombed in the shrine.

Museum of St Albans, Hatfield Road. [Telephone: 01727 819340. Website: www.stalbansmuseums.org.uk. Open all the year round. There is no admission charge.] Allows the visitor to discover the complete history of the city from its humble beginnings to its modern commuter status.

Verulamium Museum, St Michael's Street. [Telephone: 01727 751810. Website: www.stalbansmuseums.org.uk. Open all the year round. Admission charges apply.] An award-winning museum that contains superb mosaics and re-created Roman rooms, along with objects from the Roman city uncovered during excavations.

3

Norwich – 27 August 1549

British history is littered with uprisings. Some of those that were successful were led by a disenchanted aristocracy against other members of the nobility, while those that failed were often led by the masses against overbearing aristocracy. In 1549, however, a rebellion began when the English monarchy was vulnerable, and had it spread, it would have led to a very different history of Britain. So what influenced a man with land and power to give up all his privileges to fight alongside the commoner? How did an army of peasants manage to gain control of Norwich? How did they defeat the army of the Marquess of Northampton and what auspicious song of the day would contribute to their downfall? The battle of Norwich was one of the largest battles ever fought on English soil. It demonstrates the frustration that was felt by the starving peasants of Tudor England and explains what drove them in desperation to question the Government in a bid to stand up for their rights as free and just Englishmen. It forced the regency that was protecting a young and sickly king to Germany in search of an expensive and final solution.

PRELUDE TO BATTLE

Edward VI came to the throne on 28 January 1547. He was just over 9 years old and of a frail disposition, but he was a male heir of Henry VIII, and thus fulfilled his father's preoccupation with ensuring that a son inherited his throne. Henry VIII knew that he would die before Edward was old enough to govern in his own right and in his will appointed a sixteen-strong regency to support Edward until he was of age. Most of this regency were reformers, and the protector overseeing this council was none other than Edward Seymour (Edward VI's grandfather, Jane Seymour's father), though he was elected to this position by the other members of the council in direct defiance of Henry VIII's will. Edward Seymour was initially

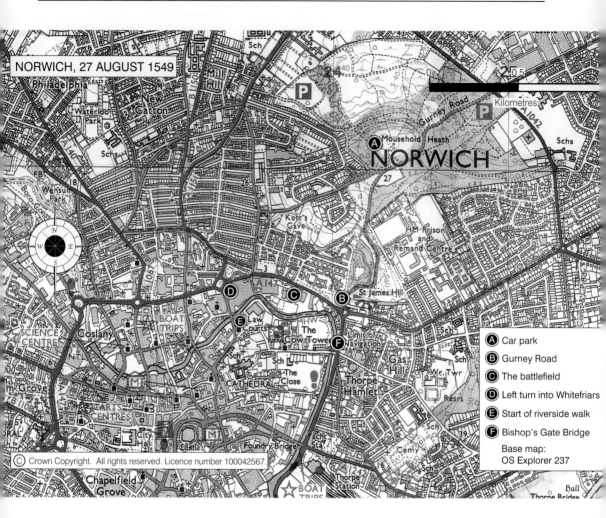

unconcerned with the plights of peasants; his aim, as protector (and the newly dubbed Duke of Somerset) was to see Edward safely, and politically, married. It was to this end that the English invaded Scotland and massacred 10,000 for the loss of just 500 Englishmen at the battle of Pinkie on 10 September 1547. This defeat, however, had no effect on the 'Auld Alliance' (the name for the long-standing alliance between Scotland and France) and gained Somerset nothing in his political scheming, as Mary, Queen of Scots, headed for France and the hand in marriage of the French Dauphin.

Ignoring the populace has always been a dubious practice and in 1549 a series of small protests began, two of which erupted into major rebellions. The first began in Cornwall, where the people, who preferred Catholic Latin or Cornish to the enforced English they could not understand in church, invaded Devon and

The market place at Wymondham where the initial seeds of rebellion were planted.

held Catholic services in Exeter Cathedral. This rebellion was brutally crushed in the village of Sampford Courtenay in Devon by the Duke of Somerset himself. The second uprising began at a summer fayre in Wymondham near Norwich and exploded into what has become known as 'Kett's Rebellion'.

The fuse for the rebellion was lit on 6 July 1549, when the annual summer fayre to celebrate the translation of St Thomas à Becket, whose chapel is in Wymondham, began. Two nights of merriment and festivities were planned and the revels were soon in full flow. Entertainment was put on, together with plays and pageants, there was food and drink in abundance and as the alcohol flowed among the locals, so did the talk. The conversation centred on their lot, the majority of which was decidedly bad. After two days of indulgence, groups formed among those people most aggrieved, and probably most addled, and they set off to destroy the enclosures and regain their common lands. One landowner whose enclosures were attacked was named John Flowerdew. To divert this mob away from his fields and those he had taken, Flowerdew paid the gang to go and pull down the enclosures that Robert Kett of Wymondham had erected. Little did he know that this 40 pence (a significant sum in those days) he paid to the mob was going to end up providing them with an inspired leader. As the crowd approached Kett's house they were met by the tanner, and

THE ENCLOSURES

Edward VI inherited a prosperous country, but one which had seen years of unchecked exploitation of the poor man by the landowning gentry. Vast areas of common lands had been enclosed and many arable fields had been turned into pasture for cattle and sheep. The well-known orator Hugh Latimer (former Bishop of Worcester) had openly spoken out against these increasing enclosures in his famous 'Sermon of the Plough'. This sermon was delivered before the court of Edward VI, and in it he denounced the nobles and gentry of England and Wales as 'enclosers, graziers and rent-raisers'. Enclosures still carried on unchecked and as the price of wool continued to rise, wool was the oil of the Middle Ages, more and more common land and arable fields were turned into sheep pasture. However, even the courts of law backed the gentry in cases throughout the Tudor, Elizabethan and even into the early Stuart periods, as the Stixwold case in 1603 testifies.

To be fair to Edward VI's father, Henry VIII had ordered direct action to stop the spread of the enclosures: he limited the amount of sheep to 2,000 per farm; and after one landowner had flattened people's houses, Henry VIII ordered him to rebuild them and to rehouse the people. But these 'punishments' against the nobles and gentry of England and Wales were few and far between. The result of these enclosures was to take away from the common man the ability to support himself. As small communities and farms disappeared, so did the infrastructure that surrounded them; the blacksmith, the tanner and the weaver all lost their livelihoods as the hamlets died. People began to starve and to migrate either to places where common land was still available, or to towns in search of work and a home. In all people there is a willingness to put up with a certain amount of injustice, but all of us also have a breaking point beyond which we are not prepared to go. The peasants only needed the right kind of charismatic leader who spoke the words they understood, and they would follow them so long as they believed things would improve, hence the number of spontaneous rebellions that erupted at times of particular hardship or injustice. All too often, though, after the rebellion had failed, the peasants were back where they started from, though fewer in number than when they began; as for the landowners, they simply kept on putting up enclosures and they continued to prosper.

when they started to tear down his fences, to their amazement he joined in. Once the task was completed, Kett found a vantage point on his property and spoke to the crowd assembled before him. It is not clear exactly what Kett said to them, but what is certain is that he was offering up himself as their leader. The words must have been both influential and charismatic, because the offer

Kett's Oak on the B1172 near Wymondham, where Kett preached to the peasants before marching on Norwich.

was one that the disorganised mob were happy to accept. With Kett now duly instated as the official leader, the mob returned to Flowerdew's lands and pulled the rest of his enclosures down.

The next day, 9 July 1549, Kett addressed a crowd that had assembled under an oak tree on Wymondham Common, close to the main road from Thetford to Norwich. Here Kett is reputed to have made another rousing speech, which apparently included the lines, 'I refuse not to sacrifice my substance, yea my very life itself, so highly do I esteem the cause in which we are engaged.' Whatever the other contents of the speech were, they clearly inspired the crowd, which now rose to a man and followed Kett on the road to Norwich. It seems, given the ease with which he was able to lead the peasants, that from the outset Kett had a clear vision of what he wanted to achieve; this was nothing more revolutionary than a fair system of government for all, where the people were able to farm their lands without the constant threat of the landowners disrupting or ruining their lives. Maybe Kett was preaching to the converted and he just happened to be the man in the right place at the right time and that is why the commoners followed him. Yet the way in which he continued to lead this growing army of people suggests that he was a fair-minded man, with great charisma and tenacity. As Kett marched on Norwich to deal with the corrupt hierarchy of Norfolk society, his ranks swelled with folk from every walk of life: not just country folk, but urban people from Lynn and Yarmouth. They ranged from stonemasons to rat-catchers and from tailors to butchers, clearly showing that it was not just agriculturally based people who were concerned with the unjust power that the gentry and nobility now wielded. On 12 July this peasant army reached Mousehold Heath. This was an area of land that Kett already had knowledge of, for upon it stood a building called Mount Surrey, which was taken and made into Kett's headquarters.

Mousehold Heath lies today, as it did in 1549, north-east of the city of Norwich and outside the city walls. This was the perfect place to encamp an army: Kett had a glorious view over the city below him, with the city walls, the cathedral and, most importantly, some of the gates and bridges clearly visible to him and his observers. From the records that remain, Kett was clearly a shrewd and capable man. He organised supplies for his army of followers, which by the end of July was estimated at being 20,000 strong. Kett first chose 2 in every 100 men to be administrators to assist in the organisation of the camp. Secondly he sent out commissioners with his official warrant, which he issued in the King's name, to every country house to provide cattle, corn and all the necessary victuals to support his men. In addition to these 'requested' goods, many smaller farmers sent in additional goods in the forms of arms, ammunition and even money. In Norfolk, the gentry feared that their days of bounty had come to an end forever.

Once Kett had established his position on Mousehold Heath, it was clear that it would need something special to draw him down from such an advantageous position. Accordingly, messages were exchanged between the Mayor and his aldermen in Norwich with the regency in London and this resulted in the arrival of a royal herald on 21 July. The herald promised that all who went quietly home would receive a king's pardon. The people, on hearing this, responded with cries of 'God save the King's majesty', but Kett knew that this talk of pardon was for the rich and famous and those who had done ill. He responded that he and his men had done nothing amiss, other than the duties of

Mousehold Heath north-east of Norwich, which the 20,000 peasants made their home.

a true subject. At this point the herald called upon the aldermen and the sword-bearer of Norwich to arrest Kett, but eight men and most of those elderly members of the town council against Kett's 20,000 was not even worth considering and the aldermen retreated into Norwich.

RECONSTRUCTING THE BATTLE

Up to this point there had been civility in the proceedings, and the gates of Norwich had been kept open for all men, including Kett's, to come and go as they pleased. The Mayor, by the name of Cow, now closed all of the gates and brought the city's guns into the meadows by the river, aiming their barrels at Mousehold Heath. This was the opening move to a protracted siege that developed over the next five weeks into one of the most incredible periods of military activity ever seen in an English city.

Kett also had a number of cannon and he had already positioned these to cover the city walls and gates below the heath. Throughout the night there were constant exchanges of gunfire between the two batteries of cannon, but there was little damage caused to either side. The next morning some of the peasants attacked the city by swimming the river, while others scaled the walls and other groups attacked the closest gates. It was at Bishop's Gate where the fighting was most fierce, but eventually the peasants broke in and within a short while were masters of the city. Seeing the situation, the royal herald again tried to intercede, but being ignored once more took his leave of the city. The Mayor and the aldermen were captured and taken to Mount Surrey, technically removing all lawfully constituted authority from Norwich, before being released unharmed and returned to the city.

The news that the royal herald carried back to London brought a swift response from the regency. The Marquess of Northampton, William Parr (brother to Catherine Parr, Henry VIII's last queen), was sent to Norwich with a small advance force of at least 1,400 men that included mounted gentry and some bill-armed levies, but the majority were Italian mercenaries. Northampton arrived in Norwich unopposed on 30 July, but within twenty-four hours his small expeditionary force was under attack. Northampton's men managed to drive off the first peasant assault, and rested that night after a day's hard fighting. But on 2 August a second assault by the peasants led to a vicious struggle on 'Palace Plain' north of the cathedral and west of the Bishop's House. This bloody battle lasted for some hours, but eventually Kett's men won the fight and, their morale shattered, Northampton and the remnants of his army fled the city. Norwich was once more under peasant control. When Somerset learned of Northampton's rout, he was furious and by the second week of August, commissions were in place in all the shires around Norfolk for the raising of the levy. Meanwhile, Somerset, who had planned to lead the relief army to Norwich himself, stepped down and allowed the Earl of Warwick to take command. There appears to be no reason available for Somerset's decision to step aside. One can speculate that at heart he may have had sympathy with the peasants' cause or, more likely given his role as protector, that he feared to be away from the young king, considering the mood within the country.

Somerset arrived at Norwich on 23 August at the head of an army between 12,000 and 14,000 in number, but his cannon were some hours behind and the 1,200 Landsknechts were a further three days away. Warwick marched into the city and once more a herald was sent to offer pardon to the peasants. They reacted as before with cries of 'God save King Edward', but the matter was soured when a young boy, making offensive gestures at the herald, was shot dead by an archer from the herald's escort. Cries of 'treason' rang from the crowd and they urged Kett not to negotiate further and not to desert them now. Kett told the herald that there could be no parley, and that he was retiring to Mousehold Heath to prepare for battle. On hearing the news, Warwick seized sixty men

Typical sixteenth-century dress, from the peasant bowmen to the armoured mercenary with halberd.

and had them hanged in the market place below the castle, 'without hearing their cause', and he sent forth a proclamation that there was a curfew, and any found out of doors would be dealt with in similar fashion. Warwick then discovered something that must have infuriated him even more: Kett's men had captured all his cannon. In a case of unbelievable stupidity, the drivers of the artillery train had entered the city at Bennett's Gate in the west, and travelled straight through the city, exiting by Bishop's Gate in the east and directly into the waiting arms of Kett's men.

Kett was now vastly superior in cannon to Warwick and set up the new cannon alongside his existing ordnance, trained upon the city below. Although Warwick cleared the city of rebels during the day of 24 August, they returned the same night, setting fire to Conisford Street, which burned for a whole day and would have spread to the entire city if heavy rains had not helped to put the flames out. Sunday 25 August was a black day for Norwich: some of the walls were beaten down, some of the gates were broken, fires raged throughout the city, troops were mustering in the open spaces and all the time the rebels prowled outside the shattered city walls. Monday 26 August brought hope to the city: the German mercenary Landsknechts arrived and on Mousehold Heath

MERCENARY TROOPS

As recently as January 2005, Mark Thatcher, son of the former British prime minister, was found guilty of attempting to involve mercenaries in Equatorial Guinea. Yet mercenaries are not just an element of modern warfare: there have always been men willing to kill if the pay is right. Persian armies that fought against Alexander the Great contained Greek mercenary Hoplites; the men of the Balearic Islands were so proficient with the sling that they served as mercenaries for both Carthage and Rome during the Punic Wars. Our own Wars of the Roses saw mercenaries from many European countries, but around 1470 a new word appeared in the German language: *Landsknecht*. By the end of the sixteenth century, this word was synonymous with a highly trained, disciplined army of mercenaries who were nothing short of a killing machine and who were willing to fight for anyone if the price was right.

The Burgundian wars of 1476–7 had shown that cavalry was now no match for the well-disciplined pike blocks that European armies were deploying. These slow-moving hedgehogs of 18ft pikes made a slow advance towards the enemy infantry, while their flanks were protected by missile troops, armed with crossbows and, of late, the new 'handgun', a type of early musket. Until artillery became more effective, there was nothing to stop the steady grind of the pike blocks. Cavalry were already vulnerable to the massed archery fire that bows and crossbows could bring, and accordingly they had become more heavily armoured to try and provide a defence against the hail of missiles which they encountered on the battlefield. This made mounted troops an expensive arm to employ in war, and Maximilian, who later succeeded to the Holy Roman Empire in 1493 as Maximilian I, was looking for a more economical way to protect his inheritance lands of the Netherlands from his rivals in Bohemia and Bavaria. He had taken note of the successful Swiss armies of the period, who were almost entirely formed from pike-carrying infantry, and he accordingly approached the *Kriegsherren*, the traditional 'gentlemen of war', in Germany who could, for the right price, provide the purchaser with large bodies of infantry, trained and capable of following the Swiss in their art of war. The commonest saying among the people who used these mercenaries was, 'no money, no Landsknechts'. This is borne out by examples of the Landsknechts on campaign. At the battle of Pavia in 1525, during the Italian wars, the Spanish general Leyva had to melt down the chalices and even his own personal gold jewellery in order to prevent his Landsknecht garrison from defecting to the French.

Initially the Landsknechts started out as mainly pike-armed infantry, but as warfare changed, these German mercenaries altered their methods, and armed their formations in line with the developments in Renaissance warfare. By the middle of the sixteenth century, their regiments consisted of a variety of differently armed troops, designed to gel together in the new battle formation, the tercio. Now only 60 per cent of a regiment's 4,000 men would consist of pikemen, 20 per cent would carry a halberd, and the remaining 20 per cent the arquebus, a type of early musket, which had begun to replace the traditional missile weapon of continental Europe, the crossbow. One elite group of Landsknechts were known as the *Doppelsoldner*; they carried a formidable two-handed sword almost two metres in length and their role was to charge into the enemies' pike ranks, slashing the ends off their weapons in order to allow the Landsknecht pikemen to close and outreach their opponents. For their pains, the *Doppelsoldner* received double the pay of their comrades.

One thing that did not change until near the end of their history was the flamboyant way in which the Landsknechts dressed. They had no uniform as such, other than to dress as garishly as possible: with slashed and open-seamed doublets, shirts and hose, one layer on top of another, they would appear as a multicoloured rainbow of an army. Various European leaders had tried in vain to impose some uniformity on their dress, but at the imperial Diet of Augsburg in 1503, their freedom of dress was granted. The Landsknechts were so highly regarded that between 1470 and 1600 they fought in many European theatres of war, employed by English, French, Spanish, Hungarian and Italian armies.

a great fire was burning. The rebels had fired their camp and were preparing for battle. The peasants had revived an old traditional song as they sat round their campfires on the heath, and some of its words were these:

> The country gnoffees, Hob, Dick and Rick, with clubs and clouted shoon,
> Shall fill the vale, of Dussindale, with slaughtered bodies soon.

Believing these words as an omen of their certain victory, the peasant army repositioned themselves on the western end of Mousehold Heath ready to attack. Dussindale was at that time a small area of land between Mousehold Heath and Norwich, and is not to be confused with the modern Dussindale Drive, a further 2 miles or so east of the city.

Warwick feared that the English shire levies might find the fight against their kin too bitter to swallow and might even end up rebelling themselves, so he left his English troops in the city with orders to prevent the rebels from entering. He then left Norwich by the north gate of St Martin's at Oak and

Bishop's Gate Bridge, the only surviving medieval bridge in Norwich. The peasants repeatedly entered the city by this bridge and Warwick's artillery unknowingly crossed over it to fall into Kett's hands.

marched east around its walls until he arrived at the foot of the heath, where he deployed his force. Before hostilities began, Warwick again offered a pardon to all who would disperse. This was the fourth time that a pardon had been offered, and once more it was rejected; the hangings in the city on Warwick's first day in Norwich gave the peasants no confidence in the nobleman's words.

From the army of 15,000 that Warwick now had at his disposal, he took all of his 1,200 Landsknecht foot; with these he would probably have had a further 500 Welsh bowmen and 500 Irish swordsmen to protect their flanks, giving him a total of 2,200 infantry. In addition, he took all of his cavalry with him, which in total, given the size of his army, would have been no less than another 1,500 men. These would have been a mixture of Reiters (heavy cavalry armed with sword and pistols), heavily armed gendarmes with lance and mace, and light cavalry armed with an assortment of spears, javelins and cross-bows. Against this highly trained and disciplined force, Kett had around 20,000 peasants armed with a variety of weapons, many of which would have been gained as a result of their earlier victories. But these peasants were not highly trained; it is unlikely that they were formed into cohesive units all armed with the same weapon. They were brave, fit men who knew how to fight in a guerrilla or ambush style, but not how to tackle a disciplined army in a prepared battle formation.

Kett had two advantages: first he had a vast superiority in numbers, and second he had overwhelming ordnance. Unfortunately, he did not bombard Warwick's army for long enough before the headlong massed charge of his army began; the peasants were convinced that the song was right and this was their day of destiny. This may have been because the first cannon shot from the rebels is reported to have brought down the royal standard, indicating that it must have come perilously close to killing Warwick himself. Whether the peasants saw this as a sign that the day was to be theirs is pure conjecture, but from a morale point of view it must have made their spirits rise. Warwick, however, had chosen his position well. This area of gentle land was one of the few places where cavalry could manoeuvre. Ignoring the fact that the peasants had chained gentlemen prisoners to act as a human shield in front of them, the Landsknechts absorbed the peasants' charge and then began to push them back. Warwick then unleashed his cavalry, which would have attacked from their usual positions on both flanks of the infantry. The Landsknechts began their steady advance but, despite losing 3,000 men, the peasants who had survived the initial mêlée regrouped on the slopes of Mousehold Heath to fight again. Cavalry could not charge uphill and Warwick was still heavily outnumbered. Apparently, at this position, Warwick offered a king's pardon to the rebels for a fifth time, and this time it was accepted, thus preventing any further slaughter. Robert Kett fled the field but was soon captured at the village of Swannington, some eight miles to the north of Norwich, and was hanged from Norwich Castle on 7 December 1549.

THE BATTLEFIELD TODAY

The name of Kett may not be well known outside Norfolk, but within Norwich and its environs it's a surprisingly common name, the visitor will see that the streets have names connected with the events of 1549. In Norfolk the battle is also known as Dussindale, which is misleading to those unfamiliar with the events. After all, the original reason for the name Dussindale has long since passed from memory, and the battle was the culmination of a month-long siege that affected the whole of Norwich, and therefore Norwich is a far more accurate term for the battle than Dussindale. Although there has been extensive building development since the Tudor period as the city has expanded beyond its original walls, the actual landscape has not changed to any significant extent. Sadly the area below Mousehold Heath, down which the peasants made their attacks against both Norwich and the armies sent against them, is now an extensive housing estate. However, the road system that circles the old city of Norwich contains a section below Mousehold Heath called Barrack Street, which bisects the battlefield. We know that Warwick's army was drawn up on flat ground just outside the city, facing Mousehold Heath. Therefore it is most likely, given that Kett's men charged down from the heath and into the waiting pikes of Warwick's Landsknechts, that the road actually marks the front line of Warwick's army, while the reserves would be positioned where the industrial units and factories now sit, alongside the river, and from where the city's cannons had fired ineffectively up onto Mousehold Heath. The bridge that spans the river to where Bishop's Gate stood is still there, and following this route into the city brings the visitor to the cathedral, to the north of which is a small street still known as Palace Plain, which is where Northampton's men were vanquished. Scattered remnants of the city walls and towers remain; one of the finest is Cow Tower named after the Mayor who tried in vain to arrest Kett. It is probable that the Mayor watched and sweated as daily the army of Kett grew ever greater, convincing the Mayor that his days were numbered.

EXPLORING THE BATTLE SITE

Although all of the military action took place in Norwich, the visitor should begin the journey at Wymondham (Thetford and Diss OS Landranger 144), where the rebellion began. Parking is readily available in this market town and it is worth leaving the vehicle in the central car park, which is situated off Market Street, and exploring the town buildings on foot. There are numerous places for refreshments as well as places to stay if accommodation is required. Local guidebooks with walks and cycle rides can be obtained from the tourist office, which is in Market Street in the upper storey of the market place. This market place (or 'butter market', as these hexagonally shaped structures are sometimes known) is one of the two buildings that should not be missed in Wymondham. It dominates the centre of the town and stands on the site of the original market place, which was destroyed in the Wymondham fire of 1615.

Cow Tower, a bastion of Norwich's defences. It was built for cannon to be operated from the roof platform, but it proved ineffective against the rebels. Annie stands to the side and this shows the considerable height of the tower.

One can imagine the revellers from the fayre gathering around the market place throughout their weekend of festivities, much as groups of people do today. It has clearly been a focal point in Wymondham for over 700 years. The second building to visit is the Abbey Church, which is reached by descending the gentle incline of Market Street before taking a left turn into Church Street on the corner of which Becket's chapel is located. The approach to the Abbey Church is quite inspiring, for ahead is a remarkable building which has two towers that dominate the skyline. The Abbey Church is a curious combination of a west tower, erected by local parishioner funds in 1448, a central church, once the church of the abbey, and the ruined Monks' Tower, which was also originally part of the abbey before the dissolution. When the monasteries buckled beneath Henry VIII's Reformation in 1538, the Abbey Church was sold to the people of Wymondham on the understanding that they would meet the valuation set by the Crown officials, and this the local people did. The magnificence of this church and the ability of its congregation to purchase it are perhaps a reflection back to a time in the 1540s when Wymondham was the fourth-largest town in Norfolk, with only the mighty Norwich and the ports of Lynn and Yarmouth ahead of it.

Once the visit to Wymondham is complete, take the B1172 to Norwich. Shortly after leaving Wymondham and halfway to the village of Hethersett is a lay-by at which the visitor should stop. Just a few yards past this lay-by is the original Kett's Oak, the very tree that Robert Kett spoke from on 9 July 1549. The oak is still alive, despite having a hollow centre and being held together with bands of iron. Incredibly, in 1841 James Grigor in his book *A Register of Remarkable Trees* stated that the tree was in a sorry state and was 'clasped around with iron'. Despite needing props, the tree has continued to flourish for over 160 years since. From Kett's Oak, continue to Norwich along the B1172 until joining the A11 on the outskirts of Norwich, some four miles away. Follow the A11 towards the centre of Norwich until St Stephens Road ends at a large traffic island. Join the circulatory system at this point, heading left initially and proceeding in a clockwise direction until at the end of Barrack Street is a further traffic island. Turn left here into Gurney Road and follow the road as it rises onto Mousehold Heath. Just after some playing fields have appeared on your right, a car park is available on the left, close to the pavilion. This is point A on the map. The whole of the battle site can be walked from this location, a distance of around two miles, but before beginning that walk a visit to Mousehold Heath should be undertaken. To date, it is not possible to determine which of the many earthworks and ditches that criss-cross the heath were there

Wymondham Abbey Church, from which William Kett (Robert Kett's brother) was hanged on 7 December 1549.

at the time of the battle. Some are later quarry workings, but it is rewarding to imagine the peasants with their rudimentary tents slung across the earthworks to give them some protection from the August sun or rain. It is not difficult to picture the many campfires that would have shone like mini-beacons upon the higher grounds of the heath, while the aromas of cooking would have mingled with the smells raised by the work of the blacksmith, the tanner and the fletcher as they toiled to prepare the army for another day at war.

Having left Mousehold Heath, the visitor should descend Gurney Road, the route down which most of the peasant forays against Norwich would have been made, until they reach the large traffic island at the foot of the hill; this is point B on the map. The site of the final battle for Norwich on 27 August is across the flat ground to your right, now bisected by Barrack Street; this is point C on the map. The visitor should now turn right into Barrack Street; at this spot, Warwick's army would have been deployed upon the left-hand side of the road backing down to the river. Follow the road round until a left turn into Whitefriars is reached – point D on the map – having just passed the puppet theatre. After the river has been crossed, there is a left turn down to the riverside walk, point E on the map. This can be taken now, or returned to after the visitor has proceeded to the end of Whitefriars. Where Whitefriars meets Bishopgate Road and Palace Street is where the 'Palace Plain' lies. This is where the peasants crushed the remnants of the Marquess of Northampton's Italian mercenaries. Having returned to point E, proceed along the riverside walk, so passing the battle site on the opposite side of the river. This walk also passes Cow Tower before joining up to the Bishopsgate alongside a public house at the side of the Bishop's Gate bridge, point F on the map. This bridge is the one over which Warwick's artillery strayed into Kett's army, and also the gate that the peasants broke through when they assaulted the city in the earlier stages of the siege. Having crossed this bridge the visitor needs to turn left once more, so as to return to point B, the traffic island ahead, before beginning the return up Guerney Road to the car park on Mousehold Heath.

CONCLUSIONS

There were countless small disturbances in the late 1540s and, to begin with, the Duke of Somerset supported the principles and views of those protesting, including Bishop Latimer. In May 1549 Somerset himself set forth a proclamation denouncing all enclosures, and as late as 14 June 1549 he issued a general pardon to those who had taken the law into their own hands in removing or destroying them. But Kett's Rebellion was something different: it came only two weeks after a riot at Attleborough, and only four weeks after the start of the Cornish rising, and if word spread of these rebellions, who knew how long it would be before the whole of England was up in arms? Significantly, Kett's Rebellion had resulted in his gaining power of the then second city in the kingdom in order to administer his own equitable justice, blatantly flaunting his 'fair' courts in the faces of the appointed officers of the Crown. Kett was to Edward VI, and the stability of the regency, a very real threat and a danger that could not be tolerated. Somerset therefore had no political choice but to do a complete U-turn in his policy and go against his own convictions for the sake of his position and his future. It is also most likely that he feared putting down the rebellion with just an English army: what if this army were to be as inspired by Kett as the other commoners had been? The risk was too great and the rebellion had to be swiftly crushed. It was surely for this reason that Somerset called for the Landsknechts to be the mainstay of his army for the battle to regain Norwich, and the destruction of Kett's peasant army. Given Somerset's actions, Kett's Rebellion must go down in history as the most successful and the most dangerous peasant uprising the nobility of England ever faced.

LOCAL ATTRACTIONS

Norwich is a thriving busy city, around the centre of which are significant remains of the original walls. Some are easy to examine as they are alongside the pavements of the road system that circles the city centre; others are currently in the grounds of building sites and are not as accessible. The city has an excellent shopping centre, with both new and old shopping parades and streets. However, in 2005 the market square is being reconstructed, disorganising the market and also parking; the traffic flow is quite limiting, described by locals when questioned as 'chaotic'. There is a lot to see in Norwich and if you intend to spend some hours, you would be well advised to seek one of the larger car parks which lie just outside the inner road system. There are numerous places to find refreshments, and plenty of inns, hotels and guesthouses in which to stay, particularly outside the main city centre. The nearest railway station is in Norwich and the tourist information centre is located at the Forum, Millennium Plain, Norwich; telephone: 01603 727927.

Norwich Castle, Norwich city centre, Norfolk. [Telephone: 01603 493636. Website: www.museums.norfolk.gov.uk. Contact the castle for details of opening times and admission charges.] From this massive castle keep Robert Kett was hanged on 7 December 1549. Inside, the castle has excellent collections of Anglo-Saxon and Viking artefacts, detailing life in those times with hands-on displays. There are similar Egyptian and Celtic galleries. There is also information on the construction of the castle and the daily lives of the people who lived in it.

Norwich Cathedral, Norwich city centre, Norfolk. [Telephone: 01603 218321. Website: www.cathedral.org.uk. Contact the cathedral for details of opening times and admission charges.] The cathedral is one of the finest Romanesque buildings in Europe and contains a wealth of medieval stone sculpture and the largest monastic cloisters in England.

4

Powick Bridge – 23 September 1642

WORCESTERSHIRE – *OS Landranger 150, Worcester and The Malverns (835 524)*

Powick Bridge is one of those unique places in the world, its low stone walls bearing witness to both the beginning and the end of the military campaigns of the English Civil War. Strategically the bridge at Powick was of vital importance: it controlled the crossing of the Teme just two miles south of Worcester before the river flows on to join the Severn one mile further east of the bridge. On this narrow, stone bridge, cavalry of both the Royalist and Parliamentarian armies clashed on a warm September day in 1642. It was the first real field action of the Civil War and, out of all proportion to the size of the forces involved, the outcome began a reputation that the Royalist cavalry were invincible. It would take the Parliamentarians years to overcome their fear of the dashing Royalist horse led by Prince Rupert, the nephew of Charles I.

PRELUDE TO BATTLE

While Parliament and the King continued their discussions aimed at bringing a peaceful settlement to their differences, both sides were also preparing for war. Parliament appointed the Earl of Essex, a veteran of the Thirty Years War, as their commander-in-chief; he was an able commander but had an unfortunate tendency to allow his opponents to outmanoeuvre him, something that the Royalist generals managed to achieve on no less than four separate occasions during the first civil war, though on only one occasion did they manage to take advantage of their situation. While the Earl of Essex was busy recruiting men in the Home Counties, the King raised his standard at Nottingham the day after being joined by his flamboyant nephew, Prince Rupert of the Rhine. Prince Rupert was handed his commission as general of horse at the Hague on 15 July 1642 by the Queen herself, as Henrietta Maria had gone to the Netherlands to enlist support for her husband's cause. Prince Rupert was another veteran of the

POWICK BRIDGE, 23 SEPTEMBER 1642

0.5 1

Kilometres

(A) Powick Church

(B) Southern side of Powick Bridge

(C) The cavalry battlefield

(D) Site of 1651 boat bridge

Base map:
OS Explorer 204

Thirty Years War but had also been captured and imprisoned. Prince Rupert, however, had used his time while incarcerated well: he had studied all the texts available to him on the art of warfare. With the pretence of negotiations now removed, both Parliament and the King increased their military activity.

Although Powick Bridge was fought over twice during the Civil War, it is the battle of 1642 with which we are primarily concerned, because after some months of recruitment and minor military activity, the field armies of both the King and Parliament were converging on the West Midlands. The King continued west from Nottingham to incorporate a number of regiments into his army, which were being raised in Wales and Cheshire. In the meantime, Prince Rupert led his cavalry force south-west along the vital supply chain of the Severn valley to protect the crossings of the Severn from Shrewsbury to Worcester. Meanwhile, the Earl of Essex had formed an army from the trained bands of London, reinforced by regiments from East Anglia, and now marched north-west towards Worcester, hoping to meet up with some Parliamentarian troops from Gloucester. Colonel Brown, attempting to rendezvous with Essex at Worcester, arrived at Powick in the early hours of 23 September with a force of 1,100 cavalry and dragoons. Despite bickering from some of the Members of Parliament within his ranks, he kept the men to attention and mounted on their horses for the rest of the night. With the light of day showing no Royalist opposition in sight, Brown deployed his men across the ridge a thousand yards or so south of Powick Bridge, which is still dominated today by the tower of Powick Church. For some inexplicable reason, Brown failed to post either an observer in the tower or send a scouting party to reconnoitre the bridge ahead, either of which would have given him advance warning of any Royalist activity in the area.

While Brown spent the morning dallying around Powick Church, Prince Rupert arrived in Worcester with a mounted force of around 1,000 men, a combination of dragoons and cavalry, with the object of assessing the city and its defences. He quickly concluded that Worcester in its current state was not an easy place to defend and it would need considerable labour to make the city tenable. Therefore he ordered his men to prepare for a withdrawal west towards Ludlow and then on to Shrewsbury in order to rendezvous with King Charles's army, which was also making for Shrewsbury but via Chester, having collected the Cheshire recruits. In order to cover this manoeuvre, Prince Rupert rode to Powick Bridge, to ensure that no Parliamentarian force should fall upon their rear. Having assessed the ground, he posted dragoons along the hedges and overgrown banks of the

The lane from Powick Bridge to Powick village, held by Brown after the cavalry mêlée had started.

river, and allowed his cavalry to dismount and get some sleep in some meadows which were in a slight depression just north of the river from where the gated lane to the bridge began.

Brown was startled into action in late afternoon when news came that Essex's army was now approaching Worcester, having marched from Warwick. Brown and his subordinate, Colonel Sandys, decided that they would set off immediately to join the earl and his formidable army of around 10,000 men. Once more there were murmurings in the ranks, and eventually Nathaniel Fiennes, one of the Members of Parliament, managed to convince Brown and Sandys to send a reconnaissance party ahead to ensure that the bridge was unguarded so that the rest of the force could cross safely.

RECONSTRUCTING THE BATTLE

Fortunately Powick Bridge is not a difficult battle to piece together. Approximately a third of Prince Rupert's force were dragoons, and these were placed lining the hedges of the fields and guarding the sides of the lanes that approached the bridge on the north, or Worcester side, of the Teme. The rest of Rupert's men were resting, some asleep, some probably talking or playing dice

Powick Bridge looking from the north, Worcester side, towards Powick village, with the narrow lane beyond.

or cards. Powick Bridge was very narrow, as were the lanes that approached the river, and no more than three, possibly four, horsemen, could cross it abreast, especially at speed. Sandys advanced cautiously at first but having crossed the bridge without opposition he began to advance along the lane towards Worcester, and still seeing no sign of any Royalist troops he called for the rest of his men to follow. Sandys' advance guard now began to gallop along the lane and at that instant they were hit from all sides at point-blank range by a volley from the Royalist dragoons. Despite this murderous close-range volley, Sandys' men continued their rapid advance and swept through the gates at the end of the lane into the meadows where the Royalists were resting, and here they began to deploy for a charge.

The sound of the dragoons opening fire was sufficient to startle the Royalist cavalry into life, and Rupert, who had been resting with all of his principal officers, reacted swiftly. Before half of the Parliamentarian cavalry were out into the field, and certainly before they had had chance to form up ready to charge in the traditional manner, Rupert led his men in a rapid counter-charge. The Royalists were unformed but came on in open order,

THE CAUSES OF THE WAR

The history of the world is littered with centuries of warfare. Some wars have come about through one country's aggression towards another as the aggressor looks to expand her frontiers, perhaps stealing valuable tracts of land or mineral deposits. Other wars have been fought in the name of religion, or because the dictator of a country wanted to raise his profile among his own people and so invaded another, weaker, country. If you examine the major industrial nations of the world today, you can see that almost every country has had at one time its civil war, and some countries, like Britain, France, Italy and Spain, have had more than one. The last Spanish Civil War was fought from 1936 to 1939, which is in living memory for 30 per cent of our population. It is one thing to take up arms against a force from a neighbouring country that is invading your territory, but it is a far harder thing to take up arms against your brother, your father or your son.

So what caused the British nation to topple into civil war in 1642? In England during the 1630s, pressure had been growing for reform in three key areas of the nation's structure: religious, economic and political changes were needed if the social and constitutional fabric of England and Wales was to hold together. These three elements are so entwined with each other that they cannot be regarded in isolation when trying to understand what led to the outbreak of the war. For political change, Parliament had long asked the King to consider their grievances about the way the country was run; eventually Parliament drew up its 'Grand Remonstrance', a list of its grievances with the King and his counsellors. King Charles I, however, mistrusted Parliament, and had ruled for many years without calling a parliament at all. The inability of Charles I to compromise and allow any parliamentary reform meant that ultimately some sort of showdown would occur.

With regard to the matter of religion, seventeenth-century Britain was a deeply secular place; as people went about their work and recreation they saw the 'goodness' or 'retribution' of God in everything they did. If the crops failed, if a pig died or if a child was born all of these things reflected God's 'influence' on Earth. People were averse to change and objected to the 'trash and trumpery' (as one contemporary song put it) of the Roman Catholic ceremonies. In Scotland, the religious system was based on a series of presbyteries; they had reluctantly accepted the reintroduction of bishops into Scotland under their own king James VI (James I of England), but Charles I heightened Scottish resentment by attempting to regain the bishops' lands that had fallen into the hands of Scottish nobles. In 1637 Charles then poured fuel onto this inflamed situation by attempting to introduce a liturgy. This action provoked an amazingly swift and well-coordinated response by the Scottish Church: within a matter of months in early 1638 they had passed a

National Covenant (which was rapidly accepted throughout Scotland) and declared that episcopacy was abolished. There was no longer a place for bishops in the Scottish Church. Charles I reacted by attempting to coerce the Scots into complying with his requests but the Scottish response was a military one, and an army was raised under the command of Alexander Leslie. Leslie was an experienced general who, like many British officers, had gained his experience as a mercenary in the Thirty Years War, which had raged from 1618 across the whole of western Europe, until ending in 1648. Charles I was unable to muster an army and therefore, with a Scottish army poised to invade, he had no alternative but to conclude a peace treaty with the Scots. The Treaty of Berwick was duly signed in 1639 and the First Bishops' War was over.

It is at this juncture that the significance of the economic situation amalgamated with the other two elements – religion and politics – to provide an unstable cocktail that would ultimately explode into civil war in the summer of 1642. Without Parliament, Charles could not receive sufficient income to be able to raise an army with which to invade and so gain submission from the Scots. When Charles did eventually call a parliament in April 1640, he removed the lid from a boiling cauldron of dissatisfied members that had been waiting to air their grievances for eleven years. Intransigent as ever, Charles I dismissed his Parliament again and attempted to form an army by levying forces across the whole of England and Wales. This shambolic and inept force crawled to Newcastle upon Tyne, with mutiny, desertion and anti-Catholic sentiments abounding, and was routed by the Scots at the battle of Newburn Ford on 28 August 1640, the victors following up their success by occupying Northumberland and Durham, and besieging Newcastle. Charles had no alternative but to sue for peace, but the Scots demanded compensation until a treaty could be concluded. With no money and no army Charles had no option but to recall Parliament again.

This time Parliament had the King where they wanted him, close to bankruptcy, and he was forced to listen to their demands for political reform. Eventually the Treaty of Ripon in October 1640 ended the Second Bishops' War, and the Scots gradually withdrew. However, the crisis deepened for Charles: rebellion had broken out in Ireland, and after a long sitting, Parliament passed the 'Grand Remonstrance' by 159 votes to 148. On his return from Scotland, Charles was presented with the 'Grand Remonstrance', while in the streets of London the murmurings against the King rose to audible levels. It seems that at this point Charles believed that only a fraction of the Parliament were rebelling against him, and that if he could remove these rebellious members, then a more stable and 'conservative' Parliament would be left with which he could then negotiate. Charles now took a course of action that would thrust a lighted spill into the unstable cocktail he had created at Westminster. On 4 January 1642 he entered the House of Commons with 300 soldiers, planning to arrest the 'rebellious' element, which he saw as led by five particular members: Hampden, Holles, Hesilrige, Pym and Strode; but the 'birds' he sought had already flown. It was the King's last move in London in this game for his kingdom. News of Charles's attempted coup spread like the plague and six days later, with armed civilians roaming the streets and the gates of the city shut, Charles fled north from the capital. The King was now convinced that it would require force of arms to regain his position. When he returned to London four years later it was as a prisoner of Parliament, and ultimately the sentence for his actions against his people would be death.

each man following as soon as he was mounted, and with great speed and determination they crashed into the ranks of the Parliamentarians, who were still forming up. Sandys was mortally wounded and fell from his horse in the first mêlée, and at once the heart went out of his men, who fled. Fiennes' troop fought bravely but were eventually overpowered and scattered. Fiennes himself managed to cut his way through the disordered ranks of his own side and make the lane which led back to the bridge, but only a handful of his men made it back across the river with him. The Parliamentarians were being pushed back on all fronts, with some being chased into the river, where they tried in desperation to get across, while others were chased east towards the Severn. Meanwhile, Colonel Brown, having heard and then seen the battle taking place on the other side of the river, had deployed his dragoons on either side of Powick Bridge to try and stabilise the situation and cover his cavalry as they tried to escape from the Royalist assault. Fiennes and some troopers from Sandys' companies would have been grateful to see their comrades covering their retreat. Rupert, though, on seeing the formed ranks of Brown's men on the opposite side of the Teme, called off the pursuit and the Royalists began rounding up the prisoners. Those Parliamentarian cavalry who had fled did not stop at Brown's command: instead they fled as far as Upton, before turning north-east to Pershore, where they met the Earl of Essex's own horse regiment, his lifeguards. Such was the panic in the fleeing men that Essex's own regiment became convinced that the Royalists were hot on the heels of the remnants of Brown's force and they all fled back to the earl's main army.

Powick Bridge from the north-west bank of the Teme, showing what a formidable obstacle the Teme was.

As ever, casualties are difficult to ascertain. Brigadier Peter Young and Richard Holmes in their book *The English Civil War*, published by Eyre Methuen in 1974, put the total Parliamentarian dead at a maximum of 150, including some fifteen officers (though quite a number of these would have drowned attempting to cross the river), while a maximum of eighty were taken prisoner. In contrast, the Royalists lost very few, though among the wounded were Prince Maurice, Wilmot, Dive, Lucas and one of the Byrons, all notable Royalists. This high proportion of wounds among the senior officers in the Royalist camp illustrates a key element in the battle. It is most likely that while resting the men had removed their armour, whether buff coat or metal back and breast plate, and when the musket shots rang out around the bridge there was no time for them to don their armour before the Parliamentarian cavalry would have been formed and charging. The Royalists therefore attacked in whatever they were wearing, probably just open doublets and shirts, against the fully equipped Parliamentarians. It is perhaps this fact alone that began the myth among the Parliamentary rank and file that Prince Rupert and the Royalist horse were brave and invincible. The Earl of Clarendon in his six-volume *The History of the*

Rebellion and Great Civil Wars, Oxford, 1888, quotes in volume III, pp. 236–7 that this action 'proved of great value to the King . . . it being the first action his Horse had been to, and that party of the enemy being most picked and choice men, it gave his troops great courage, and rendered the name of Prince Rupert very terrible indeed . . . [the routed Parliamentarians] in all places, talked loud of the incredible and irresistible courage of Prince Rupert and the King's Horse'.

THE BATTLEFIELD TODAY

Although the site has had recent construction quite close to it and the bridge has undergone several repairs, the building of the southern relief road to save vehicles passing through the centre of the city of Worcester has effectively isolated the bridge on the outskirts of the city suburbs and has now left it as a monument to the military action that has taken place there. Powick Bridge is still a narrow, low-walled, stone bridge, with the rapid-flowing River Teme beneath it. On the Worcester side of the bridge on the east side of the tarmacked lane that crosses it, there is a small meadow that leads east where the new road bridge that crosses the Teme heads out of Worcester. To the west of the tarmacked lane is an old mill which has recently been turned into private apartments overlooking the river. The small meadow between the two bridges is possibly part of those fields where Prince Rupert's men rested and then sprang so readily into action, and it would certainly be one of the places where the Parliamentarian cavalry would have tried to find an alternative place to cross the river, fighting desperately for their lives and considering their chances of surviving a swim across the river below them. It is clear that a considerable percentage of the casualties drowned, so it is most logical that this would have occurred for several hundred yards either side of the bridge. The banks all along this section of the Teme are steep and treacherous even today, and with hedges and trees upon them they must have been even more dangerous to negotiate. When one sees the River Teme itself from Powick Bridge, with the fast-flowing, dark, muddy waters of uncertain depth swirling beneath, the military importance of this small bridge at this particular crossing point becomes easy to understand. Looking from the Worcester side of the bridge towards the south, the Powick Ham ridge can be clearly seen, with the church tower dominant on the horizon; and Brown's failure to take advantage of the tower to keep an observation on the bridge and the approach to Worcester seems even more difficult to understand.

The right-hand wall of Powick Church tower, clearly showing the impact marks made by musket and small cannon balls.

EXPLORING THE BATTLE SITE

All of the site can be explored on foot but visitors may wish to drive between the bridge and the church, as part of the walk is alongside the busy A449, the main road from Worcester to Malvern. There are car parks on both sides of Powick Bridge and at Powick Church. Powick Church is a good place to start, as chronologically Brown was first to Powick and rested on the ridge the night before the battle; this is point A on the map. The church tower, which faces the car park, should be examined on its right-hand side, where musket and small cannon ball imprints can clearly be seen on the wall. These marks were made during the battle of Worcester, 3 September 1651, details of which are found on p. 62 in this chapter. Some of the church's edging stones show grooves which are believed to have been made by Civil War troops sharpening their swords the night before the battle, so these could have been made by either the Parliamentarians in 1642 or the Royalists in 1651, perhaps both.

From the church, proceed north towards Worcester on the A449 until the road traffic island is reached. On the left between the main roads is a narrow left turn into a car park. From here, proceed on foot along the footpath towards

THE BATTLE OF WORCESTER – 3 SEPTEMBER 1651

Along with the execution of Charles I, Parliament also abolished the House of Lords. An executive council was established to administer the country, and its members included Oliver Cromwell and Sir Thomas Fairfax. The inclusion of Fairfax was essential if the support of the army was going to be maintained but he was opposed to the content of the oath for this new council and it was only after considerable revisions that Fairfax was sworn in to the council. The Scots, however, would have no part in this council; Scotland remained a monarchy and it was the English Parliament that had executed King Charles I, who was not only the King of England, but also the King of Scotland. In addition, Parliament had also reneged on its promise of reforming the English Church along the lines of the Scottish Presbyterian system. Accordingly Prince Charles was proclaimed Charles II in Edinburgh, on 5 February 1649, and a third civil war was now inevitable.

Despite a heavy defeat for the Scots at the battle of Dunbar on 3 September 1650, which put back their plans for almost a year, the Scots eventually invaded England on 6 August 1651 with an army a little over 12,000 strong, and reached Worcester on 22 August, where 2,000 men were already assembled. With recruits having joined the army en route, and allowing for some deserters that had slipped off home along the way, Charles had a total force of around 16,000 men. Worcester had some indifferent defences to protect its eastward side, but the mighty River Severn protected the west flank of the city and, just two miles to the south, the River Teme joined the Severn near Powick. Given Charles's small army, this was an excellent site to defend against the larger Parliamentarian army that numbered as many as 28,000 troops, though some were newly raised regiments and militia. Key to the forthcoming assault on the city would be the bridges. Lambert seized Upton-upon-Severn for Parliament, giving them a river crossing below Worcester. From here, Parliamentarian troops under Fleetwood would assault Powick and the vital bridge below, while a bridge of boats would be built on the Teme halfway between Powick Bridge and the junction of the River Teme with the Severn, and a further bridge of boats across the Severn just north of where the Severn was joined by the Teme.

The battle began on 3 September, the anniversary of Dunbar, with assaults all along the Royalist defences. The Royalist rearguard first defended Powick Ham and its ridge against Fleetwood's advance, but despite a gallant defence of the church and the surrounding hamlet they were forced to take up a second line of defence on the Worcester side of Powick Bridge. To improve their chances of success, the Royalists had demolished two of the three spans, leaving only planks for their own rearguard to cross, before these were also removed. Cromwell himself assisted Fleetwood's attack by leading the assault over the bridge of boats thrown across the Severn once it was completed. Despite a gallant defence of all three positions – the ruined Powick Bridge and the two newly assembled boat bridges – the Royalists eventually fell back, fighting for every hedge and causing significant casualties in the advancing Parliamentary ranks. Charles, seeing his men being pushed back from the south and west of the city, launched a major counterattack with all of his cavalry and some unused infantry against the Parliamentarian position on Red Hill to the east of the city. Despite initial success, the attack was halted and then pushed back towards the city. It was the last tactical move of the battle. On all sides the Parliamentarian troops were now surging into the city. Those who could, including Charles, fled north towards their homes hundreds of miles away. At least 6,000 Royalists were captured and thousands lay dead, many of whom had fallen defending the river crossings. Charles eventually escaped to France after weeks spent in hiding as he was shuffled from one safe house to another. Cromwell went on to become Lord Protector and to govern England more tyrannically than Charles I ever had. On 3 September 1658, on the anniversaries of both Dunbar and Worcester, Cromwell lost the biggest of all battles, the one for his life. Does the third time pay for all?

Powick Bridge. This lane is the one down which the Parliamentarian cavalry under Sandys began to advance, and which Brown held after the battle had started on the other side of the river. Although the lane is tarmacadamed, the overgrown trees and the narrow passage give an indication of how the cavalry were restricted when fighting in such a confined space. Emerging from this lane the visitor arrives on the southern side of Powick Bridge, point B on the map. The importance of this narrow bridge is at once apparent, as the River Teme is a formidable obstacle at this point, varying between 5 and 20m in width, fast-flowing and with treacherously steep banks into the muddy waters below. On either side of the bridge, monuments have been placed to commemorate the fallen from the two battles that have taken place here.

Proceed across the bridge and note the narrowness and the low stone walls on either side. As you leave the bridge on the other side, you will see that a mill, that once relied on the river for its power, has been turned into a series of luxury apartments, but to the right there are still pastures and fields that lie between the old and the new bridge into Worcester, point C on the map. This field, next to the river, is most likely to have witnessed the majority of this cavalry battle.

Not all of the Parliamentarian troops were able to retreat down the lane, because they were deployed in the field as the Royalists attacked, and would therefore have been scattered to left and right as they tried to avoid the initial onslaught and buy time to regroup. An unknown number of Parliamentarians drowned and one can imagine them scurrying hither and thither about the fields looking for a way to cross the river, while at the same time fighting with Rupert's men, who were hard on their heels. Point D marks the place where the Parliamentarians put their bridge of boats across the Severn during the battle of Worcester in 1651. It was this bridge that allowed Cromwell to cross to the west side of the Severn and assist Fleetwood in his attack. Sadly there is no easy access to this site at present, but a public footpath runs from point B along the southern bank of the River Teme as far as the Severn bridge at 852 516, and this gives a good view of the meandering Teme before it reaches the Severn and one can imagine the lines of Scots desperately trying to save themselves from being outflanked as the Parliamentarians stormed across the rivers on their portable bridges towards them.

CONCLUSIONS

In military terms, the battle of Powick Bridge was insignificant: neither side gained any strategic advantage from the action, and the numbers of men involved were small, perhaps at most 1,200 on each side, so it was not a 'great' battle in terms of numbers. Yet there are some unique facts about this battle: it was the first real field action of the war and it was fought for control of a river crossing by cavalry on both sides. Yet almost immediately, both forces turned away from control of that river crossing, the Royalists rounding up their prisoners and retiring via Worcester towards Ludlow, the Parliamentarians retreating with such haste that they panicked their comrades when they reached their main field army. However, the most important point about this battle is not a fact, nor a tangible item that can be examined: it is a myth. The bravery that Prince Rupert and his fellow officers showed in mounting their horses and fighting against a fully protected opponent while still in their shirts created a story the like of which legends are made from. It gave the Royalist horse an 'invincible' tag, and when the later battles of the civil wars are examined, the majority of them open with the Royalist cavalry sweeping their Parliamentarian counterparts from the field. Edgehill, Hopton Heath, Roundway Down, Marston Moor and Naseby are battles where this occurred; the problem for the commanders of the Royalist forces is that they were unable to rally their cavalry

A unit of cavalry from the Fairfax Battalia re-enactment society charges into action. *(Susanne Atkin, Fairfax Battalia)*

after their initial success and bring them back to the battlefield in time to assist the Royalist foot to complete a victory. Time and again, the Royalist armies threw away the advantage they had gained and ended up losing the battle. In fact, it is arguable that the Parliamentarians did not win the first civil war; it was the Royalists who lost it.

LOCAL ATTRACTIONS

Worcester is a sizeable city and has everything a visitor would expect in terms of accommodation, shops, restaurants and entertainment. Powick, sitting just outside the environs of the city, has several public houses and a restaurant but the area does not have tearooms or toilets and the visitor should bear this in mind when planning to visit the site. The nearest railway station is in the centre of Worcester. The tourist information centre is located at the Guildhall, High Street, Worcester; telephone 01905 726311.

Worcester Cathedral. [Telephone: 01905 28854. Website: www.cofe-worcester.org.uk. Open daily 7.30 a.m.–6 p.m. There is no admission charge.] Worcester Cathedral is one of the finest in England and contains royal tombs, medieval cloisters and an ancient crypt, as well as a host of other fascinating features. The cathedral tower from which Charles II watched the battle of Worcester is open to visitors at certain times; contact the cathedral for details.

The Commandery. [Telephone: 01905 361821. Website: www.worcestercity museums.org.uk. Contact the museum for details of opening hours. There is an admission charge.] The Commandery is largely devoted to the history of the Civil War, with due reason, as the defence of the city by the Royalists was planned here. During the battle of Worcester, the Duke of Hamilton was stationed here. There are also special exhibits from time to time on topics relating to other aspects of Worcestershire.

The Greyfriars. [Telephone: 01905 23571. Website: www.nationaltrust.org.uk. Variable opening times; contact the museum before visiting. There is an admission charge.] This fine timber-framed building was originally a merchant's house built in 1480. The house contains panelled rooms complete with textiles and furnishings and outside there is an oasis of a walled garden right in the heart of the city.

Worcester Racecourse. [Telephone: 08702 202772. Website: www.worcester-racecourse.co.uk. Contact the racecourse for details of events. An admission charge applies.] For those interested in the 'sport of kings', Worcester has a splendid racecourse situated on the edge of the city and close to the River Severn.

5

Lyme – 20 April to 15 June 1644

DORSET – OS *Landranger 193, Taunton and Lyme Regis (345 925)*

The small town of Lyme, situated on the south coast of England, had always been an important port, and during the English Civil War it was a vital base for the Parliamentarian navy. Situated on the Dorset/Devon border, the town was a thorn in the side of King Charles's forces in the south-west. If captured, Lyme would be of enormous benefit to the Royalist cause, and Prince Maurice with an army of 6,000 men was duly dispatched to capture the town. It was seen as a rudimentary exercise: the town was surrounded by hills and had no curtain wall to defend it, and it was envisaged that it would fall to the first assault. Nothing could have been further from the truth and the siege of Lyme turned out to be one of the most unusual military campaigns in English history. Prince Maurice tried every strategic move he could to try to break the will of its defenders and capture the town, but the women continued to dig defences and the men kept sallying forth to drive the attackers away. But all the time the garrison's supplies were getting less and it was becoming harder for the Parliamentarian navy to land fresh supplies as the Royalist cannon focused on the harbour. The Prince was confident that he would capture 'that vile little fishing town' as his troops closed in on the defences.

PRELUDE TO BATTLE

Following the capture of Bristol, the Royalists needed a safe harbour on the Dorset coast in order to secure a complete line of strongholds across the south-west peninsula from the English Channel to the Bristol Channel. This would effectively cut off Somerset, Devon and Cornwall from the rest of England, giving the Royalists a secure and powerful base from which to build their forces for an assault on London. Lyme harbour met this requirement perfectly and its capture would assist the Royalist cause in two other ways. Firstly, Lyme was one

LYME, 20 APRIL–15 JUNE 1644

Base map:
OS Explorer 116

Ⓐ Car park
Ⓑ Start of public footpath
Ⓒ Sea front car park
Ⓓ The Cobb
Ⓔ The Mill
Ⓕ Football pitch

of the main Parliamentarian navy bases, under the command of the Earl of Warwick, from which raids were being conducted against the Royalist strongholds in the south-west; its capture would therefore remove these threats overnight. Secondly, it would provide the King with his much-needed base on the south coast into which continental supplies could be landed from France.

The harbour at the port of Lyme has been protected for centuries by a large, curved sea wall known as 'the Cobb'. The evocative stone structure that stands today has been immortalised in the films *The French Lieutenant's Woman* and *Persuasion*; however, the oldest parts of the current structure only date back to 1793, long after the Civil War. It is not clear when the first 'Cobb' was built, but it was first mentioned in 1294. In the reign of Elizabeth I, a Lord Burghley drew some sketches of the Cobb which are now to be found in the British Museum. The Cobb at that time was a semicircle in shape, formed from a frame of wooden piles which were infilled with stone. At each end of the Cobb, the defences were improved by the construction of two round stone battlements, each of which contained cannon capable of shooting through a 360-degree field of fire. The Cobb was not connected to the mainland until a causeway was built in 1756, which meant that anyone wishing to secure Lyme also had to secure the Cobb, otherwise supplies could be landed on the Cobb from the seaward side of the bay.

The Royalist army led by Prince Maurice was a collection of Irish, Cornish and Devon regiments, together with Lord Poulett's regiment. The majority of this force would have been infantry, together with as many heavy cannon as they could muster. Cavalry in this army would probably have been few as their role in a siege was minimal; their two main responsibilities were carrying messages between the besiegers' camps, normally a long, thin line of communications, and patrolling the roads that led to Lyme, effectively scouting the area to discern if any approaching Parliamentarian relief force was on the way.

The defence of Lyme was the responsibility of Colonel Robert Blake and, realising the precarious position that his town was in, he set about strengthening the defences. These consisted of earthworks with an outside ditch and, at regular intervals, blockhouses, which were wooden-framed buildings covered with soil and topped with turfs. These defences were in a poor state of repair and, given the small number of troops at his disposal – it is estimated that Blake had no more than 1,200 men – he called for the women of the town to come to its defence. Famously, the women of Lyme responded and initially helped in digging the ditches and building the blockhouses. However, they seem to have relished the work for, as the siege developed, the women began to

The town mill, now a teashop and restaurant, but in 1644 a vital building, providing flour to the besieged citizens of Lyme.

load and feed the muskets to their menfolk. So it was that when Prince Maurice arrived on the hills above Lyme on 20 April 1644, he did not find a town that was ready to capitulate; indeed as the Royalists advanced they were met with gibes and insults from the Parliamentarians, who were determined to show that they were not intimidated by the might of the Royalist force.

RECONSTRUCTING THE BATTLE

On 21 April Maurice launched his first attack on Lyme, planning to capture cottages close to the defensive works, but, anticipating this move, the defenders fired the buildings to deny their use to the Royalists. However, this shrewd move backfired and a thick smoke resulting from the fires blew towards the defences, obscuring the Royalist troops. Seizing their chance, the Royalists charged, but a volley of musket fire killed forty and deterred the rest, who retreated back to their lines. Seeing that an initial assault was not going to succeed, Maurice deployed his army in a semicircle on the hilltops that overlooked the town. This gave the Royalists the advantage of the high ground as well as a clear view over the town so that any Parliamentarian movements would be seen. Immediately, the Royalists commenced the construction of a series of artillery emplacements on the western side of Lyme from where they would have a clear shot onto the harbour and town below. The next day, Colonel Were, subordinate to Blake, led a sally against these new emplacements and succeeded in driving the Royalists back to their lines. From here on, the siege developed into a series of raids, counter-raids and sallies. Each time a new battery of guns opened fire on the town, the defenders would appear and throw more earth and turfs onto their rudimentary fortifications before sallying forth to drive the gunners away. Frustrated at the lack of progress, Maurice launched an all-out assault on the fortifications on 28 April, so determined to succeed that he even had his cavalry behind the infantry ready to follow up the breakthrough into the town. The defenders blasted the advancing Royalists with case shot, killing as many as eighty and causing others to turn and run, despite threats from their own cavalry to renew the assault. Undaunted, Maurice ordered all of his cannon to keep up an incessant fire upon the town to try and demoralise the defenders and thereby prevent any more sallies while the Royalists prepared for another assault.

Although the Parliamentarians had had the best of these initial exchanges, they were now desperately short of provisions but were saved from surrendering by a timely delivery of food and ammunition by Warwick's navy. Rearmed, the defenders sent forth another sally against the Royalists' western battery, once more silencing it. Maurice, seeing that the defenders' forts were the key to the town's defence, began constructing his own fort opposite the largest Parliamentarian blockhouse, Davey's Fort. On 5 May a letter was sent by sea to Parliament, requesting a relief force be sent by land to save Lyme, as there was no guarantee that the navy would be able to keep the town supplied. On 6 May a thick fog came and enveloped the town and all day the defenders expected an attack. Eventually, at around 7 o'clock, when Maurice reckoned that the defenders would have retired for supper, he launched another series of attacks, all of which failed and left at least another eighty Royalists dead. To make matters worse, fresh supplies were delivered on 11 May together with 300 men, reinforcements for the garrison.

Realising that the harbour and its protective Cobb were now the key to the capture of Lyme, the Royalist artillerymen moved three large cannon and a host of smaller ones to the west side of Lyme on what is now Devonshire Head. From this new position, which was completed by 15 May, Maurice could bring shot to bear on both the gate that defended the Cobb and on the shipping that lay at anchor in the harbour. After three days of silence, the stillness was rocked as a battery of no less than sixteen guns began to rain shot into the harbour. After

Lyme Regis Football Club ground, the most likely site of Davey's Fort, which resisted all Prince Maurice's attempts to capture it.

several days of intermittent bombardments, the defenders sallied from the town again and drove back the Royalist gunners, succeeding in capturing some ammunition, baggage and a number of prisoners.

The frustration felt by Maurice at these continual setbacks must have been immense, as he decided to go for yet another direct assault. On 21 May, though no source indicates how it was achieved, as many as sixty Royalists succeeded in

ARMIES IN THE CIVIL WAR (1) – THE HORSE OR CAVALRY

Cavalry was split into three types. The majority, some 90 per cent of the mounted troops, were heavy cavalry. They were protected with either a back and breastplate or a strong leather buff coat, sometimes both. For offence they were armed with a sword, carbine and pistols. Their tactic was to ride up to the enemy foot, discharge their carbines and pistols and then retreat to the rear of their regiment to reload, before advancing again to repeat the process, a tactic known as the 'caracole'. Once it was thought that these 'softening' tactics had worked against their target unit, the cavalry would then charge home to drive that enemy unit from the field, creating a gap in the enemy's line which the cavalry could then exploit by attacking the now unprotected enemy rear. At the outset of the Civil War, the Parliamentarian cavalry fought in this way, according to the drill book. It was Prince Rupert who was to challenge this theory dramatically, and it began with his devastating success at Powick Bridge (see chapter 4). Having seen the success of a cavalry charge in action, he taught all of the Royalist cavalry to charge the enemy, firing their pistols at close range as they closed for combat, rather than the rhythmic caracole so favoured on the continent. This simple but dynamic tactic served the Royalist cavalry well throughout all of the civil wars, and time and again they drove the enemy cavalry from the field. What let them down was their inability to rally after their initial success and so return to the battle behind the enemy lines and complete the victory over the isolated Parliamentarian infantry. It was Oliver Cromwell who succeeded in training the Parliamentary cavalry to rally after the charge and return to the battle in time to make a decisive impact. This is arguably Cromwell's greatest individual achievement, because at both Marston Moor and Naseby he succeeded in turning what looked to be a certain defeat into an overwhelming victory, with Naseby guaranteeing that Parliament would defeat the King.

The second type of horse were the dragoons. These men were more lightly equipped than the rest of the horse and were mounted on the poorest of animals. They were attired as musketeers and were effectively mounted infantry, though some did have a flintlock musket, which was more reliable and accurate than the crude matchlock that the infantry used. In battle they often dismounted and protected the flanks of the heavier cavalry by lining hedges, walls and woods, firing in support of them.

As stated earlier, at the outset of the war some regiments were equipped from the estates of the landed gentry. This led to a third type of cavalryman, the cuirassier, who rode into battle in a full suit of armour. This armour was not the plate mail of Arthurian legend or the Wars of the Roses, but a flexible armour that allowed the man to move and shoot from the saddle; it was designed to protect the horseman while he caracoled against the enemy. The advantage was that in the charge these heavy horsemen could deliver a crushing impact on the enemy, especially if they were against cavalry more lightly armed. The cuirassier had slowly disappeared from the wars on the continent, but certainly at the start of the English Civil War there were several regiments formed from private armouries. On the Parliamentarian side it is certain that Sir Arthur Hesilrige, and possibly the Earl of Essex's lifeguard, were cuirassier regiments, while in the King's army it seems probable that his personal lifeguard and the regiment of the Earl of Northampton wore full armour.

getting into the harbour area. As no assault on the defences is recorded, one must assume that this was achieved by the use of a number of small boats, perhaps setting off from Pinhay Bay or Charton Bay, both of which lie a few miles to the west of Lyme. The first indication to the garrison that their defences had been breached was when flames were seen coming from the boats set alight by Maurice's men. The Royalists, having caused considerable destruction, then fought a desperate battle to escape. They eventually retreated but found the Parliamentarian defenders pursuing. Seizing his opportunity, Maurice countercharged with his cavalry, who must have been placed to cover the retreat of his raiding party. So successful was this cavalry attack that the Parliamentarians were driven all the way back to the quay, where the Royalists were able to complete their attack on the shipping.

ARTILLERY IN THE CIVIL WAR

Artillery was broadly split into two types: that used in the 'field', i.e. in battle, and that required for a siege.

The poor state of the roads made troop movements difficult enough, but moving artillery was a nightmare. This meant than an army on the march would have only a handful of cannon with them and these would range from a light gun such as a fawcon firing a ball of 2.5lb in weight, to a culverin firing a ball of 19lb in weight. The commonest field guns were the sakers, which weighed just short of a ton each, but could be handled by six men and pulled by a team of six horses, and shoot a distance of a mile. All of these cannon were muzzle-loading and required a team of people working together to ensure that they could be operated effectively and safely. The first thing was to clean the gun barrel with a wet sponge before a drying wad was used to remove any excess damp; then the gunpowder would be scooped from the wooden barrel and ladled into the gun barrel before a small piece of wadding was pushed home; next, the cannon ball would be dropped into the gun barrel; and finally a wad of earth or cloth would be rammed home to secure the ball and the powder in place. After the sponging, a 'powder monkey', normally a young lad, would have his finger over the touch-hole to ensure that no air could get to the powder during loading and so cause an explosion. Then from a separate horn, the master gunner would pour gunpowder into the touch-hole. To fire the cannon, a piece of smouldering cord was simply plunged into the naked powder via a linstock. A linstock was a simple wooden pole some six feet in length which had a metal sprue designed for holding a length of lighted match; this meant that the cannon could be fired from a safe distance. Once fired, the gun would be sponged clean and the whole process would begin again.

Siege artillery pieces were fired in exactly the same way, but these massive cannon were capable of shooting cannon balls weighing as much as 50lb a distance of almost a mile. Siege cannon could weigh anything from two to four tons and require sixteen or more horses to pull them along. Mortars, the Renaissance equivalent of the howitzer, were capable of firing explosive hollow shells as well as solid cannon balls and had the advantage that they could fire over walls and obstacles because of their high trajectory. Cannon balls were made of solid iron, but as they did not explode they only caused damage if they actually hit something. However, because of the style of fighting during the seventeenth century, the targets were solid blocks of infantry and cavalry, a large target formed up six or more ranks deep. One hit on the front rank could therefore kill or maim six or more people. At the first battle of Newbury on 20 September 1643, the artillery caused significant casualties on both sides: a Royalist ensign, John Gwyn, recorded that he had seen 'a whole file of men, six deep, with all their heads struck off by one cannon shot of ours' (Young and Holmes, *English Civil War*, p. 149). An artillery train would make up no more than 5 per cent of an army on the march.

Even a small field-piece cannon such as a saker could fire a ball for well over a thousand yards. Siege pieces were capable of shooting twice as far with a shot four times heavier. *(Susanne Atkin, Fairfax Battalia)*

Lyme was now in a desperate position and, on 23 May, Blake rowed out to meet Warwick to discuss the situation. Warwick then sailed east towards Charmouth, a hamlet two miles along the coast, and pretended to land troops there. Initially this bluff succeeded but a Royalist cavalry patrol would soon have confirmed that the ships were merely creating a feint to draw off the Royalists. Sensing victory Maurice launched a ferocious artillery barrage against the western defences and at last created a breach in them. Determined to get into Lyme, a thousand men were sent to exploit the breach but, undaunted, the defenders held out. Three times the Royalists came on, and three times they were repulsed, reputedly losing 400 casualties to those Lyme men and women who were determined not to give ground.

Maurice was exhausted as all of his attempts had failed, but among his men were Irish regiments, some of whom still carried the longbow as a missile weapon. It seems that now, in desperation, the Prince decided to try an old-fashioned method of siege warfare and he called for these bowmen to shoot fire-arrows into the town. Once more, luck was not on the Royalists' side: they succeeded in setting fire to a number of houses but the breeze was blowing from the sea and carried the sparks away from the town. Although twenty houses were destroyed, Lyme was still defendable. Now, between 24 May and 12 June, there appear few records of any action from the besiegers, though Warwick wrote a letter on 12 June clamouring for the urgent dispatch of a land-based relief force, stating that 'the enemy were daily approaching nearer and nearer [to the town]' and he was risking much in supplying the daily needs of the garrison. It seems then that for three weeks Maurice had decided to try and dig siege trenches to allow his men to get close to the earthworks without risking the high casualties of an assault across open ground. However, while the siege had been in progress, Parliament had been responding to the letter sent on 5 May and it had issued orders to the Earl of Essex to the effect that either he or Waller should march and relieve the town. On 12 June Maurice received news that Essex and his army were closing in on them from Blandford and regretfully he had no alternative but to issue orders for the siege to be lifted.

One can imagine the enormous sense of relief that must have flowed through the tired limbs of the people and garrison of Lyme. As the Royalists packed up their camps, the Parliamentarian cannon played on them, adding further injury to an army that Warwick estimated had lost 2,000 men, 40 per cent of its force. In comparison, the Parliamentarians lost a mere 120 people, but it is not known how many of the brave women were among them.

THE BATTLEFIELD TODAY

Sadly, after the end of the first civil war, Parliament ordered that all of the earthworks be levelled to prevent their future use. The slighting of all defences save for those castles and estates wholly loyal to Parliament, occurred all over England and Wales and accounts for many of the ruins visited by people today. It is unclear exactly where the majority of the forts were constructed or where the earthworks ran, but despite these drawbacks it is possible by piecing the evidence together to produce a picture of where the key points of the siege took place. Brigadier Peter Young concluded that there were four forts protecting the outer defences, of which Newell's and Davey's were the two most important (P. Young and W. Emberton, *Sieges of the Great Civil War*, Bell, 1978, p. 66). The most important point for Lyme was its harbour and protective Cobb. Therefore there must have been a fort on the west end of Lyme to protect this vital artery of supply, from which a ring of earthworks ran, punctuated every few hundred yards by a blockhouse, which would normally be constructed to guard a route into the town. This defensive ring would have continued around the perimeter of the town until the coast was reached on the east side.

At the far east of Lyme Regis, until the middle part of the twentieth century, a road ran along the coast to Charmouth, but this road and the cliffs for several hundred metres inland have now been eroded away. Clearly there would have been a fort to guard this coast road, and this is believed to have been 'Newell's Fort'. The other key fort was Davey's, apparently named after the man who was responsible for its defence against the Royalist attacks. This is known to have been next inland from Newell's Fort and was subjected to repeated attacks, so it was seen as the key to the landward side defences; it was this fort that prompted Prince Maurice to construct Fort Royal opposite to try and weaken its position. Local tradition has it that Davey's Fort is where Lyme Regis football pitch now lies, which is logical, since Newell's Fort would have been on the coastline immediately south of this location. Given that the land was levelled by Parliament it is interesting to note that before the football pitch was constructed, the ground was one continual slope towards the sea, upon which allotments had stood for many years. Apparently, gardeners digging in the allotments found the occasional musket ball and other Civil War artefacts upon the site.

Although the successful defence of Lyme ultimately rested on the Cobb, the existing structure does not date back to the Civil War. However, it marks where the original one stood as far as anyone can tell and it provides the visitor with

The Cobb, seen from the cliffs at the western end of Lyme Regis, indicating the kind of view that the Royalist gunners would have had when bombarding the harbour with cannon shot.

the chance to stand and contemplate the view that Warwick's sailors had of the siege. One can imagine that, as they landed their supplies to be transported into the town, they would have seen the plumes of smoke rise on the hills above it, followed by the heavy 'boom' of the gun just before the cannonball thudded into the harbour – if they were lucky, simply soaking them and their provisions in the process.

EXPLORING THE BATTLE SITE

The locations important in this battle are easily explored on foot, and most of the walks are on pavements or public footpaths across fields. However, Lyme Regis is a hilly place with steep roads and steps in places, so strong shoes are recommended. For those not able to walk long distances, it is possible to park at the first and last points on the map, and drive between them as required. The most central place to park is at point A on the map, at the top of Pound Street. Once the vehicle is parked, proceed back to the vehicular entrance and turn left, walking up Sidmouth Road, the A3052, going away from the sea. After a few hundred yards, turn left into Ware Lane and follow this until there is a sharp left and right turn, followed by a small gate on the left, which opens onto a public footpath, point B on the map. The visitor is now standing on Devonshire Head and between here and the cliffs below, the Royalists set up their large battery to attack shipping in the harbour to the east of them. Descend along the fence line and follow the signposts that appear for the Cobb. About halfway to the Cobb, a footpath will appear on the left which returns through 'Pine Walk' back to the car park. From this point, much of the descent is down steps and through trees and there are excellent views of the harbour and Cobb below. It is easy to imagine the Royalists using such a route to try to surprise the fort that would have protected the harbour below. This path emerges by the town's bowling club and ahead is the large seafront car park, point C on the map. Follow the road round to the harbour and ahead is the Cobb, point D on the map. Care should be taken when walking on the Cobb walls, as the top layer slopes towards the open sea and there are no guardrails. In rough weather, the waves can break right over the Cobb, both a spectacular sight and a danger to keep clear of. Once the visit to the Cobb is completed, return along the harbour to the mainland and take the promenade walk towards Lyme town centre.

Lyme Regis looking from the Cobb. The solid groyne on the far left of the picture indicates where local historians have uncovered musket balls. The sloping ground at the far right is where, since 1950, much of the cliffs has eroded and where, during the siege, Newell's Fort would have been located.

Looking down onto the beach below, especially if the tide is well out, allows areas of rocks to be seen among the sand. There is a large area known as Lucy's Ledge, and as one looks to the right of this there is a smaller section of rock. Amateur historian Roy Gollop, whose son keeps the aquarium on the Cobb, has used a metal detector within the Lyme area for many years. On one occasion on this unnamed ledge of rocks he found a hatful of musket balls, possibly small cannon balls. There are several ways in which these projectiles could have become embedded in the rock and, most likely as they were found all together, they were fired by one artillery piece. As cannon protected the Cobb, it is feasible that these small shot were fired at the Royalists on the night they managed to attack the shipping in the harbour. More mundanely, it could just be that a bucket or small sack of musket balls destined for the musketeers defending the town was lost overboard when supplies were being delivered and they sank as one onto the rocks below; either way such finds after 350 years bring the Civil War and the battle for Lyme to life.

At the end of the promenade turn up and right into Bridge Street, using the road bridge to cross the River Lim. Take the next left, Coombe Street, then left again into Mill Lane. The square at the end of Mill Lane is point E on the map and the mill, which would have been of vital importance for the defenders during the siege, is still visible for the visitor to see, though today it is a tearoom. The millrace and green are a lovely area to explore, but ultimately the visitor should return to Bridge Street and turn left into Church Street. This road eventually runs into Charmouth Road, and there is a steady ascent for the majority of this section. After several hundred yards, a car park will appear on the right, followed by the entrance to Lyme Regis Football Club, the pitch being point F on the map. This is the most probable location for Davey's Fort. Now walk east as far as it is possible to go on either the car park or the football ground; this allows a view across some remaining allotments and out to the open sea. It is difficult to imagine as one looks out to sea that the land once continued for many hundreds of yards and that Newell's Fort once sat protecting the Charmouth Road. Retrace your steps from here all the way back to Bridge Street, before ascending Broad Street and then turning left at the top of this shopping street into Pound Street. After a few hundred yards, you will return to point A, the car park.

CONCLUSIONS

The inability of Prince Maurice to break the resistance of the people of Lyme and complete the Royalist domination of the south-west of England was a serious blow to the King's cause. It also broke the reputation of the Prince, who was personally depressed after the failure of his campaign. Maurice's increasing desperation, but also his ingenuity, is shown by the varied ways in which the town was attacked: open assaults, bombardments, fire arrows, trenches and counter-forts were all tried, so one cannot criticise his endeavours. The most surprising thing is that, having succeeded in getting onto the quay twice in one evening, the Royalists failed to press home their advantage, but perhaps Blake moved more of his garrison to the western and Cobb Gates, knowing that the Cobb was their lifeline and therefore required the most protection. Lyme illustrates perfectly that the key to any successful siege is cutting off the defenders from food, water and ammunition. The loss of any of these three vital elements is sufficient to render the town or castle undefendable. The importance of the navy being under the control of Parliament was ultimately the deciding factor at Lyme, because Warwick was able to supply the defenders, their morale remained high and they were able to withstand the harrowing barrages and direct assaults from Prince Maurice's men.

LOCAL ATTRACTIONS

Lyme Regis, as it is now known, still has a bustling port but it is tourism that is now the major income for the town, though fishing boats still operate and freshly caught fish are available throughout the year. There are a wealth of places to stay ranging from hotels, through guest houses to inns, as well as numerous places to eat and a fair selection of shops, including some excellent bookshops. Lyme Regis is part of the newly termed 'Jurassic Coast', and accordingly Lyme Regis and its neighbouring towns and villages now have shops dedicated to the collection and sale of fossils. The nearest railway station is at Axminster. The tourist information centre is located at the Guildhall, Church Street, Lyme Regis; telephone: 01297 442138.

The Jurassic Coast. [No telephone number. Website: www.jurassiccoast.com. Open during daylight hours. No admission charge.] An area of coastline that extends for ninety-five miles along the southern coast of England between Exmouth in Devon and Studland in Dorset. This unique area contains geological time-beds from the Cretaceous, Jurassic and Triassic time periods. Guided walks are available at some of the locations and fossils can be found on many of the beaches in the area. It is worth checking with the local tourist office as well as with the website.

Lyme Regis Aquarium. [Telephone: 01297 444230. No website at present. Contact the aquarium for opening times. There is an admission charge.] Situated out on the Cobb, from which there are fine views back across the harbour to Lyme Regis. The aquarium contains an exciting range of ever-changing local sea creatures, including the remarkable hairy sea mouse.

Lyme Regis Philpot Museum. [Telephone: 01297 443370. Website: www.lymeregis museum.co.uk. Contact the museum for opening times. There is an admission charge.] Based in Bridge Street, overlooking the sea. Contained inside is a wealth of information on the history of Lyme and its people, together with award-winning displays of the geology and fossils of the area.

Montgomery – 18 September 1644

POWYS – OS *Landranger 137, Ludlow and Church Stretton, Wenlock Edge (221 969)*

Montgomery has clearly always been a strategically important place: a Roman marching fort, an Iron Age hill fort and Norman earthworks are all still visible in the hills that surround the ruined thirteenth-century castle. Though always a small town, its geographical position, lying just a few miles south of the River Severn at Abermule, and roughly halfway between Newtown and Welshpool, was vital to any army seeking to control the Marches of Wales and the supply route through the Severn valley. Indeed in medieval times Montgomery was traditionally the place where the English and Welsh lords met to parley. In 1644, following an almost farcical succession of circumstances, one of the largest battles ever fought in Wales took place on the outskirts of the town, and set in progress a series of events that had a major impact on the first civil war. In many respects, Montgomery would turn out to be a greater blow to Charles I than the disaster of Marston Moor, yet Montgomery is excluded from many printed volumes that claim to be the 'complete' guide to British battlefields.

PRELUDE TO BATTLE

Montgomery Castle, although a ruin, sits proudly high above the town, dominating the lands below it. At the time of the Civil War it was a key link in the Royalist supply chain: convoys of troops from Ireland and both troops and supplies from Wales would regularly pass on the road that runs alongside the River Severn a few miles away from the safety of the castle. Wales had long been the nursery for many of the King's infantry regiments and it was natural that eventually Parliament would turn its attention to this part of the kingdom. The reason that Wales was the last area on Parliament's list was its location. Much of the Parliamentarian support was in the Home Counties and East Anglia, as far

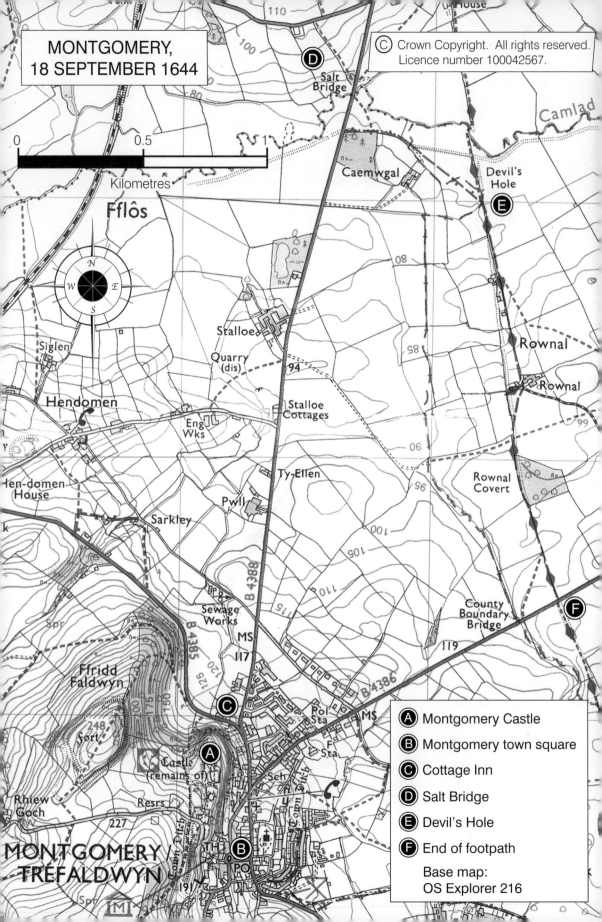

MONTGOMERY,
18 SEPTEMBER 1644

Camlad

Salt
Bridge

D

Caemwgal

Devil's
Hole

E

0   0.5   1

Kilometres

08

Fflôs

Rownal

N
W E
S

Stalloe

98

85

Rownal

Siglen

Quarry
(dis)

94

Hendomen

Stalloe
Cottages

06

99

Eng
Wks

Ty-Ellen

96

Rownal
Covert

Hen-domen
House

Pwll

Sarkley

100

105

County
Boundary
Bridge

F

Sewage
Works

MS
117

110
115

119

Ffridd
Faldwyn

120
125
175
150

B 4385

B 4388

B 4386

248
Fort

C

Pol
Sta

MS

A

Castle
(remains of)

Sch

Ff
Sta

Rhiew
Goch

Resrs

227

B

PO

A	Montgomery Castle
B	Montgomery town square
C	Cottage Inn
D	Salt Bridge
E	Devil's Hole
F	End of footpath

Base map:
OS Explorer 216

MONTGOMERY /
TREFALDWYN

191

Montgomery Castle, built on a natural rock promontory, was a formidable defensive location.

away from Wales as it is possible to get. Taking any decisive action against Wales was extremely difficult as it meant marching an army across the breadth of Britain and through territory in the south and west Midlands which was Royalist in sympathy, and into Wales itself, which was almost entirely Welsh in sympathy. It therefore fell to local Parliamentarians to begin the action against Wales to see if they could make an impression without any help from London.

The local Parliamentarian generals were Sir Thomas Middleton and his brother-in-law, Colonel Thomas Mytton. Middleton was exiled from his home in Chirk Castle (Clwyd) early in the war when the Royalists under Robert Ellice captured the castle in his absence. He was therefore happy to accept a commission from Parliament to become responsible for all the military action on their behalf in north Wales. Mytton was from Halston, an estate outside Oswestry, and he established the first Parliamentary garrison in Shropshire when he captured Wem in 1643. Mytton then went on to capture Ellesmere and Oswestry, at last giving the Parliamentarians a supply line towards Wales. Buoyed by their success, Middleton and Mytton began to increase their patrols south from Oswestry towards Welshpool and Shrewsbury and the all-important Severn valley. In late August 1644 a company of Prince Rupert's horse were attacked and routed at Welshpool, losing many horses in the attack. The Prince himself was on his way to Cornwall to confer with the King, leaving the garrison at Montgomery to protect the area.

ARMIES IN THE CIVIL WAR (2) – THE FOOT OR INFANTRY

There were four basic troop types in the Civil War and for any army to operate successfully it was important that these different troop types fought as integrated components of the whole, the fear being that if one troop type became isolated then it would be vulnerable to an attack from an integrated force. There were, of course, exceptions where troops of only one type were involved, as the 'all-horse' affair of Powick Bridge indicates.

Musketeers on a defensive dyke hold off a combined attack from a traditional infantry regiment, musketeers flanking the pikemen in the centre. *(Susanne Atkin, Fairfax Battalia)*

The foot, or infantry, would make up about 75 per cent of an army. The men would be formed into regiments, each in theory consisting of 1,200 men, 800 armed with muskets and 400 with pikes. The pikeman was armed with either a buff coat and a back and breastplate, sometimes both, as well as a morion-type helmet. The musketeer at best had a buff coat for protection, but often would be in just his shirt and doublet. If they were lucky, they might all have a uniform coat colour. Such was the nature of the Civil War that very few regiments ever reached their theoretical number and some regiments had as few as 400 men. The role of the musketeer was to shoot as many of the enemy as possible, softening them up before the pikemen advanced and drove the enemy from the field. The musketeers would be formed up in many ranks, possibly ten or more. They would then advance and fire, while the line that had just discharged their muskets would retire to the rear, slowly reloading their musket as they advanced through the files ready to fire again. Thus, in theory, a never-ending series of volleys could be discharged at the enemy, one line after another. The reason for this cumbersome system of firing was the appalling inaccuracy of these muzzle-loaded, smooth-bore weapons, the only effective way to hurt your enemy being to bring a lot of firepower to bear upon them at a range of a hundred yards or less. It would not take long for the musketeers to discharge all of their shot, as generally they had only enough ammunition and powder for twelve shots, normally carried in a bandolier worn across the shoulder and chest and commonly known as the 'twelve apostles'. Once all of the shot was discharged, it was common for the musketeers to join in the charge alongside their pikemen, using the hard shoulder-stock of their musket as a club.

However, the role of the pikeman was not only an offensive one. The pike was no more than a glorified spear, anything from 12 to 18ft in length, and carried by men who generally had some body protection. The musketeers were vulnerable to attack, especially from enemy horsemen, while they went through the cumbersome system of loading and firing and rotating their ranks. The pikemen could therefore offer protection to their musketeers by keeping the enemy horsemen from engaging with them, as the cavalry would not charge home against the densely formed pike ranks.

When the war began, the King held few centres of industry, as Bristol, Norwich and London, the three key cities of the day, were all held by Parliament. Hence Royalist regiments were reliant on what equipment was stored in the personal homes of the King's supporters. When the war began in earnest, the majority of men within the Royalist regiments were armed solely with pikes, and some of the rear ranks had to be content with cudgels. Gradually, as a result of victories in the field and the eventual capture of Bristol in August 1643, the King was able to equip his foot with better weapons and, interestingly, it was the musket that was adopted by the infantry rather than the pike. Indeed by the time of Naseby, 14 June 1645, the Royalist foot regiments were almost entirely armed with muskets, indicating that the days of the cumbersome pike were numbered.

In contrast, the Parliamentarians, by gaining control of London at the outset of the war, had a ready-made army of foot, namely the trained band regiments that were designed for the defence of the capital. The army of Parliament under the command of the Earl of Essex was able to use the armouries that supplied these trained bands and equip their regiments in the proper manner of the time, with the correct proportions of musket to pike, a ratio of 2:1. However, despite the proven successes that Montrose and the later Royalist armies had had in using a far-higher ratio of muskets to pike, when the New Model Army was formed under Thomas Fairfax in 1645, he chose to stick with the drill books of the day and kept the ratio of two musketeers to each pikeman.

Mytton, having been temporarily abandoned by Middleton, now found himself besieged by a large Royalist force, which had been swelled to almost 5,000 troops by the arrival of the experienced regiments of Lord Byron's army. The Royalist infantry began digging trenches and earthworks around the castle in a concerted effort to regain the stronghold as quickly as possible. Meanwhile, Middleton's relief column had been placed under the command of the experienced Sir John Meldrum and his force of around 3,000 men reached the outskirts of Montgomery on 17 September. Byron took up an excellent position high above the castle on Ffridd Faldwyn Hill (216 969). This gave him a clear view of the siege unfolding below him and allowed him to monitor all the approach roads to the town. Having seen the advance of Meldrum's men from the north, Byron gave orders for all of his men to be brought back to the town and he deployed them on the high ground around the town. Meldrum retained his men in readiness of an assault and, having arrived from the north, positioned his army in the fields on the eastern side of 'Salt Bridge' a little over a mile from the town. Protecting this bridge ensured that the Parliamentarians had a means of escape should one be required, while the River Camlad would protect their rear. Also, Offa's Dyke ran to the east of their position and it's most likely that Meldrum would have patrolled this to ensure no attack came from that direction.

RECONSTRUCTING THE BATTLE

The night of the 17th passed without incident and on the morning of 18 September Meldrum, seeing no movement from the Royalist troops stationed on the hills above, decided to send 500 of his cavalry in search of provisions. Byron from his vantage point saw some of the Parliamentary horse leaving their camp and, sensing that the moment was right to strike, assembled his men and marched down through the town. The Royalist army would have attacked almost due north from Montgomery, heading towards the defensive position that Meldrum had adopted the night before. Given that Meldrum's force was at least 2,000 less than Byron's, especially since he had reduced his cavalry by the 500 men sent foraging, it is most likely that Meldrum would have stayed in his defensive overnight location. Using his considerable experience, Meldrum would have occupied Offa's Dyke to his left with his infantry and defended the vital crossing of the Camlad, Salt Bridge, with his cavalry on his right. In the centre would have been the rest of his infantry and any light cannon that the army had with them. This would have made a formidable defensive position, but gamely

Salt Bridge, which the Parliamentarian cavalry fought desperately to hold in the initial Royalist charge.

the Royalists came on at full pelt. Meldrum said in his later account of the battle that the Royalist cavalry under Colonel Marcus Trevor charged into our horse 'with great courage, resolving to breake through our Forces and make themselves Masters of a Bridge we had gained the night before, which would have cut-off our retreat'. (J.E. Tomley, 'The Castle of Montgomery', *Archaeologia Cambrensis*, combined edition, undated, p. 29). Clearly this is Salt Bridge, confirming where Meldrum's cavalry had been deployed and indicating that both sides grasped the importance of controlling the bridge. In this battle, Sir William Fairfax was mortally wounded and the Parliamentarian cavalry began to give ground. Against the Parliamentarian infantry Byron's men were also making progress, but Brereton's Cheshire infantry regiment refused to give ground and the impetus of the Royalist charge was halted.

At this crucial phase of the battle two incidents occurred which were to influence the outcome. Firstly, Mytton and his 500 men surged out from the castle, assaulted the Royalists still engaged in the siege and, having routed them, descended the steep hill to the town and attacked the rear of the Royalist reserves. This panicked the remaining Royalists, and a furious Trevor maintained afterwards that the Royalist 'Lancashire Horse ran without a blow being struck' (*Archaeologia Cambrensis* (1846) 37–8, (1849) 237–8). Secondly, the Parliamentary foraging party returned, bringing 500 cavalry back into the fray as the infantry were locked in their titanic struggle along the whole line of battle. With cries of woe from the Royalists as Mytton fell upon their rear, and panic among the cavalry as the returning Parliamentary horse joined the battle, Brereton's Cheshire 'Lions' suddenly broke through Byron's line. From what only twenty minutes earlier had seemed a certain victory, the Royalists collapsed to a humiliating defeat.

Byron's army was completely destroyed; as few as 100 infantry made it back to the safety of Shrewsbury. At least 500 were killed, and perhaps as many as 1,500 were taken prisoner. The cavalry had been scattered to the four winds. Crucially, all the baggage, cannon, supplies and weapons were lost. The Parliamentarians lost only forty men, with another sixty wounded, according to Brereton, but given that the Royalists had the upper hand particularly in the initial cavalry mêlée for Salt Bridge, these seem unduly low casualty figures; no doubt propaganda played no small part in all of the generals' reports that came out about this battle. Sir William Fairfax died the next day as a result of the dozen wounds he had received in the battle. A Major Fitz-Simons was the only other notable casualty.

The Battlefield Today

In 1982 the author was fortunate enough to visit the excavations at Montgomery Castle and was able to confer with the then current senior archaeologist for Wales. The author was shown over 250 musket and pistol balls that had been discovered, together with coin and rings from the Civil War period, some in mint condition. The majority of the projectiles were found close to the southern walls of the castle; as there had been no shots from the Parliamentarian troops when they captured the castle, this indicates that this shot was from Royalist troops concentrating their firing around the gateway of the castle, which Mytton was reinforcing. From a military aspect, there were two important finds outside the castle. Firstly, evidence emerged of an artillery battery that had been set up on Ffridd Faldwyn west of the castle. Presumably this was Byron's vantage point, mentioned above. At this site, a series of small wooden blocks used for the production of musket balls were found, together with an actual row of cast musket balls lying where they had been set to cool after casting more than 350 years ago. During the

THE 'ENGLISH' CIVIL WAR?

The very title for this period of British history is misleading, as firstly there was not one but a whole series of civil wars and, secondly, although the majority of these military campaigns raged across England, there was also fighting in Ireland, Wales, Scotland and even in some of the colonies.

There were in fact three separate 'British Civil Wars', punctuated at times by periods of peace. The first civil war was the most destructive, lasting from August 1642 to August 1646 and involving hundreds of sieges and skirmishes, and more than fifteen major engagements. The second civil war lasted from March to August 1648, and was more a series of isolated uprisings than a full-blown war. The third civil war lasted from June 1650 to September 1651 and came about as a direct result of Parliament's actions after the end of the second civil war. Firstly, Parliament had reneged on its promise to reform the English Church into the Scottish Presbyterian system and, secondly, they executed King Charles I, who was also the King of Scotland. The Scots had fought alongside Parliament to 'release the King from his evil counsellors', not to have him murdered. So, on hearing the news that Charles I had been executed, there was disbelief and annoyance in Scotland, and therefore Prince Charles was proclaimed Charles II in Edinburgh, on 5 February 1649. The first attempt at restoring Charles II to the throne met with disaster at the battle of Dunbar on 3 September 1650. But despite this defeat, the Scots remained undaunted and gathered their forces for an invasion of England, which took place in the summer of 1651. The Scottish and Royalist army eventually reached Worcester where it was soundly beaten by Oliver Cromwell on 3 September 1651. Charles's dream of obtaining the throne was gone, but at least after nine years of almost continual warfare, Worcester turned out to be the last military action of the 'English' civil wars.

excavations, ponds, ditches and other damp drainage areas around the town and the battle site were dredged and in one of these a complete lobster-pot helmet, normally worn by cavalrymen, emerged from the mud; upon closer examination, the helmet was found still to contain the skull of its original owner, the victim seemingly having had his head cleanly severed from his neck during the battle.

Given the evidence above, there can be little dispute as to the area across which the battle of Montgomery was fought. The cavalry battle ebbed and flowed on the right wing of Meldrum's army as they vied for control of Salt Bridge, while east of the bridge the infantry held the advancing Royalists long enough to allow his foraging cavalry to return and Mytton to launch his rear attack from the castle. Meldrum was then able to leave his defended position and commence his own counterattack, and the Royalists, engaged on three sides, crumbled into submission. The battle then would have been fought in a square formed by the following points: Stalloe Cottages at 224 982; Salt Bridge at 227 994; Devil's Hole (is this perhaps a reference to severe fighting that took place here?) at 232 992; and Rownal at 234 983. The Royalists would have advanced past Stalloe Cottages, charging steadily downhill to the Parliamentarians, who occupied the two sides of the square formed by the three points of Salt Bridge, Devil's Hole and Rownal.

EXPLORING THE BATTLE SITE

The site lends itself to exploration on foot and the walker will be traversing ground that has changed little since the Civil War days. Beyond Montgomery town centre, parts of the site can be explored by vehicle, but there is limited parking and the section along Offa's Dyke can only be walked. As the cause of the battle lay in the loss of Montgomery Castle, the ruins of this once-proud stronghold is the ideal place to begin. The castle is clearly signed from the town; for vehicles, a winding road takes the driver up onto the castle plateau, while for those on foot there is also a steep footpath. The castle is located at point A on the map and there is a free car park at the entrance. The ruins are in a good state of repair and are well worth exploring as there are signboards giving further information about the castle. From the north wall of the castle the Camlad valley and the roads that converge at Montgomery can clearly be seen. This confirms that Mytton would have had an excellent view of the battle unfolding below him, so allowing him to intervene on his comrades' side at the crucial moment. Once the castle has been explored either descend by foot into the town itself or return via the vehicle road. There is plenty of free car parking within the town itself, so those people wishing to avoid the steep descent from the castle may wish to return to the town square, point B on the map, and leave their vehicle there.

From the town square, either of the two roads that head north can be used to proceed to the end of the town; the castle now towers above you on the left. A sharp bend in the road junction ahead has the B4385 heading to Abermule and Newtown. This should be ignored and the visitor should take the steep right turn, next to the Cottage Inn, which is the B4388 to Welshpool at point C on the map. None of the B-roads listed have footpaths once they have left the town boundary and care should be taken when walking along them. The road goes straight for over a mile before arriving at Salt Bridge, which, Meldrum knew, had to be defended to ensure that his army had an escape route if the battle went against them; this is point D on the map. The fields to either side and south of the bridge are the most likely scenes of the opening cavalry battle in which the Royalists had the initial advantage. Examining the River Camlad which flows under Salt Bridge indicates why this small river was such a formidable obstacle: the waters are too wide to leap and the steep banks and unknown depth of water mean that it was difficult for infantry to ford without risking their lives.

From Salt Bridge retrace your steps back towards Montgomery, and just before the woodland there is a gate on the eastern side of the road. Take this public footpath which then bends in a gentle arc for about a third of a mile around the back of Caemwgal Farm, before joining Offa's Dyke path near Devil's Hole at point E on the map; at this point the visitor is standing on the left flank of Meldrum's army where his infantry would have waited for the arrival of Byron's men charging downhill from Montgomery. Having joined Offa's Dyke path, follow this south for another third of a mile until reaching the derelict buildings around Rownal. The infantry battle is most likely to have raged on the fields to your right, for the whole of this distance, before Meldrum's men would have left their defensive positions and driven the Royalists back towards Montgomery.

Just after Rownal but still on Offa's Dyke path, continue south for another half a mile until a gate indicates that you have reached the B4386; this is point F on the map. Turn right onto this road and just over half a mile later you are back in Montgomery with a short walk to the town square. The complete walk, starting and finishing at the castle, is almost five miles but the only steep sections are the ascent to and descent from the castle.

CONCLUSIONS

The defence of Montgomery is in sharp contrast to that of Lyme, and it is interesting to compare the fortunes of these two strongholds: Lyme, which had poor defences, managed to hold out through the determination of its people, and Montgomery, which was well ordered for defence, was given away through apathy. It is very rare that a single action can determine the outcome of a whole war, yet the events of Montgomery in the summer of 1644 were to prove an absolute disaster for the King. The escalating series of events that had begun with the loss of a convoy of ammunition then led to the loss of Montgomery

The battle site viewed from Offa's Dyke at Rownal. This is the most southerly position to which Meldrum's troops woud have deployed.

Castle, which caused an experienced field army to be drawn out as a relief force into a battle in which it was totally destroyed. After the loss of Montgomery Castle, the stream of recruits that Wales had supplied to the Royalist regiments all but disappeared and the supply convoys could no longer carry vital armaments and food to the Royalist armies and garrisons in the west of England. Byron's field army of 5,000 men would have been invaluable in the Midlands, especially the following year at Naseby, because that battle was close to being a Royalist victory and those extra 5,000 men could have made all the difference. To the best of the author's knowledge, the battle of Montgomery has never appeared in any books on British battlefields; yet Montgomery is probably the largest battle ever fought in Wales and it was a defeat from which the Royalists never recovered and therefore its significance should not be underestimated.

LOCAL ATTRACTIONS

Montgomery is still a small town, with a very gentle easygoing air. There is a small range of places to eat: teashops, restaurants and several inns, and a selection of small local shops. It is hard to imagine from its size that it was once the county town for Montgomeryshire, but lying as it does at the convergence of key roads from Shrewsbury, Welshpool and Ludlow and guarding the important Severn valley, its prominence was founded almost 1,000 years ago when it was an important Norman stronghold guarding the dangerous border with the then hostile Wales. The nearest railway station is to be found at either Welshpool or Newtown. The nearest tourist information centre is located at Vicarage Gardens, Welshpool; telephone: 01938 552043.

Montgomery Castle. [No telephone number. Website: www.cadw.wales.gov.uk. The castle is open at any reasonable time. There is no admission charge.] With a specific car park, the castle is easy to visit and the main paths are quite flat, though the perimeters are quite uneven in places and care needs to be taken, especially if children are present. The site contains excellent site boards that give the history of the castle and there is a specific plaque that gives details of the battle itself.

Dolforwyn Castle. [No telephone number. Website: www.cadw.wales.gov.uk. The castle is open all the year round. There is no admission charge.] This castle is located about four miles west of Montgomery and, like Montgomery, is in the care of CADW, the society for the care of Welsh monuments. This castle was built under the orders of Llywelyn ap Gruffudd as a direct snub to the English lords who had forbidden him to build it, even though it was in Wales and not England. Llywelyn retorted that in his own country he would build what he liked. However, when those same English lords besieged it in 1277, the castle surrendered on terms after just one day. The castle is located near Abermule, some three miles north-east of Newtown, and is signposted at the same location as Dolforwyn Hall, turning left off the A483 Newtown to Welshpool road. Follow the signs to the castle and there is a specific car park on a ridge below it. Dolforwyn Castle is reached by a long ascent of half a mile, which is along farm tracks and lanes. The ground around the castle is quite undulating and care needs to be taken, especially if children are present. The site contains excellent site boards that give the history of the castle.

The Old Bell Museum, Montgomery. [Telephone: 01686 668313. No website. Contact the museum for opening hours. There is an admission charge.] An excellent country museum with the history of the town and the Cambrian Railway.

7

Inverlochy – 2 February 1645

INVERNESS-SHIRE – OS *Landranger 41, Ben Nevis, Fort William and Glen Coe* *(118 751)*

From the moment James Graham, Marquis of Montrose raised his standard at Blair Atholl on 28 August 1644 the course of the Civil War in Scotland changed. No longer could Parliament rely on an ever-increasing number of troops to support their war against the King in England. Despite being ill equipped, with few provisions and fighting against armies double and triple the size of his own, Montrose fought and triumphed in a series of brilliant military campaigns that criss-crossed Scotland, leaving ruin and death in his wake. While Montrose prevailed, King Charles had hope. Inverlochy is today, as it was in 1645, a tiny community nestling between Loch Linnhe to the west, the ruins of the long-abandoned medieval Inverlochy Castle to the north and the mighty Nevis range to the east, but it lends its name to a battle which was the climax to one of the most incredible and daring military campaigns in British history, through which Montrose once more outwitted his opponents and won the chance to confront another of the armies that stood in his way.

PRELUDE TO BATTLE

When Montrose arrived in Scotland he formed an army that was made up of Highland clans, loyal to the Stuart cause, and men who had been trained to fight from an early age and were masters of the Highland charge. The rest of his army were Irish troops, most of whom were particularly fine musketeers trained to fire salvos before charging home, and they were all battle-hardened veterans, capable of enduring hardship; they were as tough as their Highland comrades. Marching from Blair Atholl, Montrose crossed west to Inveraray on Loch Fyne and then north around the coast, up through Glen Coe, over the mountains to the Laggan glen and then once more up the coast to Killcummin at the base of Loch Ness. All the time he was on the move, Montrose knew that the Covenanter (see p. 57)

INVERLOCHY, 2 FEBRUARY 1645

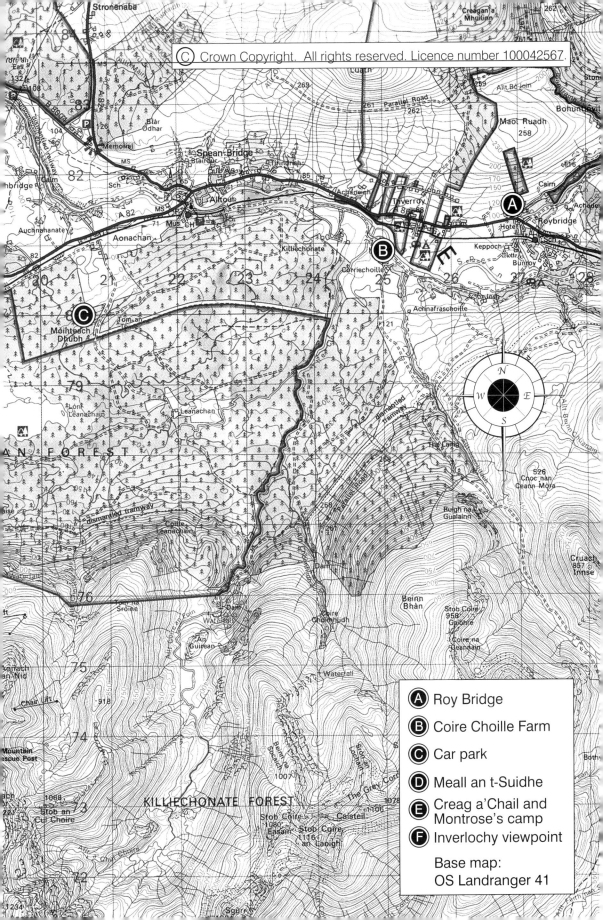

(A) Roy Bridge

(B) Coire Choille Farm

(C) Car park

(D) Meall an t-Suidhe

(E) Creag a'Chail and Montrose's camp

(F) Inverlochy viewpoint

Base map:
OS Landranger 41

armies were trying to corner him between them. To the south was the army of the Marquis of Argyll, and the might of the Clan Campbell with a force of around 3,000 men, many of them experienced soldiers. Coming from Perth to trap Montrose from the north was Major General William Baillie with a second Covenanter army almost 5,000 strong.

At Killcummin, Montrose learned that the two armies were just sixty miles apart, and he was in the middle, with conceivably no way out, for the highest mountains in Britain hemmed him in on both the east and west sides of the valley. The Campbells were south at Inverlochy near Fort William, and Baillie was north at Inverness straight up the long Loch Ness. All that Montrose had was a force of 1,500 men, but although his troops were sound, he knew that they could not take on two armies in opposite directions at the same time as well as being outnumbered at five to one.

Montrose now discussed an audacious plan. He proposed turning back south so as to confront the smaller of the two armies sent against him, but although it was smaller, he knew that the Campbells were the superior force in terms of military strength. This was because at this time the Clan Campbell was like a separate country within Scotland, controlling vast rich pastures filled with farmsteads and cattle. The family was wealthy and had experience in a wider world by virtue of their proximity to the sea and the fact that they invested in the education of their sons at university, away from their traditional homeland. Their troops were well trained and well armed and bore a hatred for some of the clans represented in Montrose's army, which meant that they were eager for a fight. The fellow officers in Montrose's army were in full support of his plan, though it meant marching through high passes during the depths of winter with few provisions to support them.

So the Royalist army turned south, marching to Lochaber and Glen Roy, reaching their first destination in just a day and a half, having covered a distance of some twenty or so miles. Montrose then set out from Roy Bridge in Glen Spean on the morning of 1 February 1645 to begin his march south-west. He travelled along the River Spean to a point below Inverroy, where he crossed the river by a ford at 253 807 close to Coire Choille Farm (Corriechoille House according to John Buchan in his 1928 book, *Montrose*). From here, still heading south-west, Montrose and his army started to ascend the slopes of the Nevis range, heading towards Ben Nevis. At this point where Montrose crossed the River Spean, the bed of the river is formed of layers of solid rock, some slightly jagged, others worn smooth by the constant erosion. This natural phenomenon occurs for hundreds of metres along the valley floor, providing a natural stone

Roy Bridge, from which Montrose and his army embarked upon their incredible march.

pavement as the riverbed. On visiting the site, even after weeks of rain and snowfall, the author found the river fordable by either stepping onto the exposed rocks or onto the many large stones that lie scattered across this wide riverbed. To the battle-hardened troops of Montrose's army, the River Spean presented no obstacle. From the ford, Montrose made his way west for half a mile to Killiechonate at 242 811, before turning south-south-west and marching for two miles until he reached Leanachan House at 220 786.

From Leanachan House, Montrose followed a series of local tracks and paths around the lower slopes of Ben Nevis, which took him in a south-western arc to Torlundy at 145 772, from where he headed due south to the lower slopes of Meall an t-Suidhe at 139 730. The written evidence quoted in Buchan clearly states that Montrose, having travelled at the head of his men, then waited for the rest of his army to arrive before setting up camp on the lower slopes of Meall an t-Suidhe; their staggered arrival took a further three hours. Montrose's position overlooked Loch Eil, which meant that they had to be in the vicinity of Creag a'Chail at 136 744, because further west or east from there and the view would have been impaired. This location gave Montrose a commanding view of Loch Eil, the flat land around Inverlochy Castle, and, most importantly, a view of all the roads that met at Inverlochy from Glen Nevis to the south-east, from

MARQUIS OF MONTROSE

James Graham was entitled as the Marquis of Montrose on 6 May 1644. His brilliant campaign that resulted from this appointment, as he struggled in vain to bring an army to the assistance of Charles in England, is the most remarkable of the whole Civil War. Indeed, if Charles II had had someone of his calibre pitted against Cromwell and the New Model Army, the outcome of either Dunbar or Worcester could have been very different.

In 1638 Montrose, along with the vast majority of Scots, had subscribed to the Covenant in direct opposition to Charles I, and he joined the Scottish armies that fought and defeated the English in the Bishops' Wars of 1639 and 1640. However, Montrose became disillusioned with the Covenanters as their policies and ideas became more and more extreme, and in 1642 he changed his allegiance to Charles I. Initially Charles I was sceptical, showing once again, as throughout his reign, his indecisiveness. This incapacity to make a decision and abide by it, coupled with his extreme stubbornness go a long way to explaining Charles's inability to reason with any opinion contrary to his own. The many years that Charles chose to rule without calling Parliament are a prime example of his character.

Accordingly, it was 1644 before Charles I showed any belief in Montrose's ability and this occurred while Montrose was at court, in the desperate Royalist capital of Oxford, where disease and the stalemate in the war had brought the morale of all to a very low ebb. Charles saw little to be gained by pampering and supporting this 'youth' and his extravagant claim that he would raise Scotland for the King. After all, the Covenanters held every town and city in Scotland, and with the Parliament, the Church and the nobility firmly behind them they controlled every avenue to recruitment. But most importantly of all, they controlled the purse strings; it is easy to see why Charles I thought that there would be neither money nor recruits for Montrose in Scotland.

Montrose's reply was brutally straightforward: 'I will not distrust God's assistance in such a righteous cause, and if it shall please your Majesty to lay your commands upon me for this purpose, your affairs will at any rate be in no worse case than they are at present, even if I should not succeed' (Buchan, *Montrose*, p. 162). The King chose to listen to Montrose and agreed with his simple requests. Lord Antrim, himself only recently escaped from captivity, was to raise 2,000 troops in Ireland and the isles, and these men were to be landed on the west coast of Scotland to act as bait to keep the Earl of Argyll occupied. This would then give sufficient time for Montrose, aided by cavalry from Newcastle's army, to break through the Covenanter lines that guarded the Scottish Borders and reach the comparative safety of the Highlands. There was also talk of the King of Denmark sending German mercenary cavalry to support Montrose. In order not to upset his superiors, in both rank and age, Montrose was happy to take the title of lieutenant-general, which was conferred upon him on 1 February 1644. Charles issued instructions to match Montrose's requests and agreed that arms and ammunition must somehow be transported to the north to equip this new Royalist army in the Scottish Highlands. It was with a glad heart that Montrose rode north in March 1644.

Loch Leven to the south-west, from the Great Glen to the north-east and from Glenfinnan to the west. Despite his desire for surprise, there was some sporadic shooting between the pickets of both sides, but incredibly the Campbells believed that they must be a few Royalist scouts. They considered that it was impossible for Montrose and his army to have travelled to Inverlochy through the mountains in such atrocious winter conditions, which consisted of snowdrifts and ravines on the ground while avalanches and cornices of ice hung overhead, the whole being described as 'deathly cold' at night (J. Buchan, *Montrose*, Thomas Nelson and Sons, 1928, p. 223). Given these conditions and

The River Spean at Coire Choille, where Montrose forded the river to begin his climb towards Ben Nevis.

only cold porridge to eat, it is a wonder that Montrose had any army left, let alone one prepared to charge an enemy army at dawn.

Meanwhile, the Marquis of Argyll decided to retire to his ship out on Loch Eil; he was confident that his second in command, Sir Duncan Campbell of Auchinbreck, could honour both the Covenanter and Campbell cause, and deal with any threat from this token force which that Royalist upstart had sent south.

RECONSTRUCTING THE BATTLE

Sir Duncan Campbell must have been amazed to see the whole of Montrose's army high upon the hills above him, but his defensive position was a strong one, and he had the advantage of ground and twice as many men as Montrose commanded. The historical website www.scotwars.com contains information on the battle of Inverlochy and states that Campbell 'placed his men in four divisions along a ridge of firm ground running roughly north–south'. This frontage was formed from a mixture of Lowland and Highland Scots, while in the rear was another Highland unit together with two artillery field pieces. In addition, this website also confirms that the army when deployed was 'only a stone's throw from Inverlochy castle' and that some fifty musketeers were placed there, presumably to protect the left flank of the army. Meanwhile, the Royalists were eager to commence the battle, especially as some of them had scores to settle with the Campbells, standing in the centre of the Covenanter line. The Royalists simply deployed in two battalions. The Highlanders, in traditional loyalty, were under the command of their respective clan chiefs. Montrose, close to the royal standard, was with Ogilvie's troop of cavalry, while in the centre of the army were the Irish musketeers under the command of Colonel James MacDonald (O'Neill's Regiment). Not surprisingly, given the route they had taken, they had no cannon to deploy.

The battle began with the blood-curdling cries of the Highlanders as they swept down the hills across the narrow valley floor and then, just before they reached the enemy, the Irish let forth a volley into their enemy which was so closely delivered 'that they gave it in their breath' [Buchan, *Montrose*, 1928, p. 226] before crashing into the Covenanter line. The Lowland men ran at once; the Highland regiments also retreated, but in the confusion they crashed into their own reserves, who in turn began to leave the battle. It was over in less time than it takes to tell, 3,000 men blown away by one close-range volley during one savage charge; but then the killing began.

The Ordnance Survey places the battle at 118 754, just north of the viewpoint and close to Inverlochy Castle. Contrary to this, the tourist office in

The ridge upon which the Covenanter army stood is now topped with a small memorial to the battle.

Fort William advises visitors that the battle site lies beneath the industrial works that run alongside the A82 from Claggan north to the aluminium works, and possibly both are right after a fashion. The most important fact then in determining where the action occurred is not where the battle started but where it ended. We know that the Covenanters were chased into the loch and north into Inverlochy Castle tower, and crucially that 'most scattered along the shore, and on that blue February noon, there was a fierce slaughter from the Mouth of Nevis to the narrows of Loch Leven' (J. Buchan, *Montrose*, p. 227). This confirms that the battle must have been fought at the base of the ridge, which is where the main A82 road now runs. The Royalists would have charged down from Creag a'Chail, across the industrial areas of Claggan and where the aluminium works now stand, before crashing into the Covenanters' line around the small ridge through which bedrock is clearly visible, indicating that the ridge is a natural feature and not man-made. This ground can be clearly seen by looking south-east from the viewpoint, with the main road below and the works and wasteland beyond, but it is not a pretty view. As Montrose's Royalists drove back the Covenanters, they would have fled towards the point where Loch Eil and Loch Linnhe meet, across the ground on which the modern Inverlochy

THE ARMIES OF SCOTLAND DURING THE CIVIL WAR

The formation of the Covenanters' armies was based on the training manuals of the time, many reflecting the tactics developed and used with great effect by the Swede Gustavus Adolphus as he campaigned for the Protestants during the Thirty Years War, 1618–48. In this they mirrored the Royalist and Parliamentarian armies and an army would ideally consist of 75 per cent infantry, 20 per cent cavalry and 5 per cent artillery. The Scottish armies of the time, however, had elements not seen south of the border. At least half of the Scottish cavalry would carry the lance, a weapon that had died out in England many years before. There would also be a proportion of Highlanders present, possibly forming as much as 25 per cent of the infantry. They would be armed with weapons that were seen as outdated in modern seventeenth-century warfare: the two-handed sword (the claymore) and the longbow. Many Highlanders would carry a shield, axes, pistols and knives as well as the occasional musket. Although these weapons seem archaic when set against the disciplined regiments of western European armies, one has to remember the terrain and the environment that the Highlanders fought in. The Covenanter armies were therefore a bridge between the two types of warfare, the old and the new. In contrast, the army that Montrose led was contrary to any training manuals of the time, and among the tens of similarly formed armies across western Europe was totally unique.

Montrose led an army recruited from Ireland and the highlands and islands of Scotland. Artillery and cavalry made up no more than 5 per cent of the total army; indeed the lack of quality horse troops in Scotland was something that would hinder the Stuart cause in Scotland for the next hundred years. Montrose's strength lay in his infantry, which broadly consisted of two types, musketeers and Highlanders, which comprised in roughly equal proportions the remaining 95 per cent of the army. The musketeers were made up of Irish and Gordon foot, and the former were trained to fire salvos, rather than using the rotation system to shoot into the enemy. Both regiments were also capable of using their swords in the traditional Highlander manner, which meant that a deadly salvo of close-range musket fire could be followed up instantaneously by a vicious charge. The rest of the army was Highlanders, often sworn clan enemies of those Highlanders fighting on the Covenanter side. In appearance, arms and tactics these Highlanders were almost identical, for the majority carried the claymore as their principal weapon, together with a shield, perhaps an axe, a pistol or two, a knife and sometimes a musket. Interestingly, in Montrose's army as many as half of his Highlanders carried the longbow, including a unit of around 300 led by a Commander Kilpont.

Montrose's men relied on their initial salvo to shatter the enemy, such as displayed by this re-enactment group. *(Susanne Atkin, Fairfax Battalia)*

Although Montrose was always outnumbered, his military strategy ensured that when his army was deployed he was able to make maximum use of the local terrain and so nullify the superior numbers arrayed against him by the Covenanters. He could not, however, continue performing miracles without replacements for the few men he lost and the ammunition and supplies he used. At Philiphaugh, Montrose was caught off guard by 4,000 men led by David Leslie. Despite fighting bravely and losing 50 per cent of their men in battle, the Irish troops surrendered and Montrose fled back to the Highlands with no more than fifty men, all that remained of his gallant army. Despite assurances made to the Irish when they surrendered, every Irish person taken prisoner, whether man, woman or child, was killed en route to their confinement – just one in a long list of atrocities that occurred increasingly towards the end of the wars.

houses now stand; hence, Montrose Square, at the centre of this housing estate, is aptly named. Finding themselves trapped between the pursuing Royalists and the icy waters of the loch, some fled south along the loch side for up to fifteen miles [Buchan as above], and suffered 'a fierce slaughter'. Others tried in vain to swim to the galley of their chief, which was now fleeing before any boats could be commandeered by Montrose to begin a nautical pursuit. The western

Camerons, who had lined up with the Covenanters, though at best it was a dubious alliance, now changed sides and joined in the pursuit and slaughter of their recent allies. Such was the speed of Montrose's victory that he recorded only eight dead from his army, though Sir Thomas Ogilvie was one of them. The massacre of Covenanters and especially the Campbells was brutal, with over 1,500 slain, and it was only exhaustion that eventually stopped the slaughter and allowed a few of the Campbells to escape.

THE BATTLEFIELD TODAY

The importance of this battle site lies not only in the eventual battle, which was a stunning victory for the Royalists, but in the manner in which Montrose managed to position his troops to give himself a chance of victory when only three days before, his enemies must have presumed that they would be completely crushing Montrose and his small army. Fortunately the circulatory route that Montrose took from Roy Bridge to Inverlochy is largely untouched. True, there are ski centres, and much forestation, but the important locations mentioned on the route are still there to be seen, with the benefit of beautiful scenery as a backdrop. The battle site of Inverlochy itself is now squeezed into the narrow ridge, which was the Covenanters' position at the start of the battle. In front of the ridge across which Montrose's men would have charged is an industrial site with works on either side. Where the A82 runs below the ridge is the most likely point where the two armies came into contact, the lay-by being on that mêlée line. Behind the ridge, a railway line and the streets and squares of Inverlochy mark where the Covenanters ran and were pursued to the edges of Loch Linnhe by Montrose's jubilant Irish and Highlanders. Fortunately Inverlochy Castle is still standing and the ruins where some of Campbell's men were stationed are easily accessible. The location is an enviable one and must have been beautiful before the encroachment of modern housing and industry.

EXPLORING THE BATTLE SITE

The visitor to this area will experience some of the most beautiful and unspoilt scenery to be found in Britain. Given the brilliance of Montrose's campaign, it is worth exploring all of the key places upon that epic march so as to appreciate just what Montrose achieved. It is possible to explore the whole of this campaign on foot, but a combination of driving to the relevant sites and then walking is probably best, unless a full day's walking along the route taken is the

The ruins of Inverlochy Castle, in which Sir Duncan Campbell posted some of his men to protect his left flank.

plan. The author's visit coincided with blizzards and piercing northerly winds, capturing the exact conditions that Montrose and his army had endured with nothing to sustain them but cold porridge and water. One can only marvel at the hardships these brave Highlanders endured to follow a man and a cause in which they believed.

In order to follow in Montrose's footsteps to Inverlochy it is necessary to commence at Roy Bridge in Glen Spean at 273 813; this is point A on the map. It was from here on the morning of 1 February 1645 that Montrose began his march south-west, following the river valley. To reach the ford that Montrose used to cross the river, take the A86 west from Roy Bridge until you arrive at Spean Bridge. Take a left turn after crossing the stone bridge, which is signposted for the local railway station. Ignore the actual turn to the railway station which is on the right and veer left following a minor road which runs through a large forest parallel to the River Spean, heading east. After approximately two miles you will cross Cour Bridge and after another half a mile the road ends at Coire Choille Farm, point B on the map. There are places to park throughout this route and the area is perfect for exploring on foot or to partake of a picnic.

Retracing your steps will bring you to Montrose's next landmark, half a mile west at Killiechonate, 242 811. It is possible to walk from Killiechonate to Leanachan House at 220 786, as a path leads through the forest south along the

Cour river for just over a mile, before turning west towards Leanachan. Alternatively the visitor can follow the minor road back to Spean Bridge, and then proceed west towards Fort William on the A86. Follow the main road for almost a mile, before a crossroads will be seen on the left-hand side, just after a series of six or so dwellings. The turning to the left is into a single-tracked road that only leads to Leanachan, a distance of just over two miles. There is a large Forestry Commission car park two-thirds of the way along the road, point C on the map, and this is an excellent place to stop and explore the rest of the journey to Leanachan House on foot. The house is still lived in today, and the current owner was able to confirm to the author that Montrose did indeed pass through the house, resting a short while before continuing. This is borne out not only by the traditional history of the house, but also by the discovery of artefacts, including a coin from the period, in the grounds of the house.

From Leanachan a series of tracks and paths take the walker west towards the Nevis ski centre at 172 774, and so on via Torlundy at 145 772, to the Victoria Bridge at 124 757, and thence to the Inverlochy viewpoint at 118 750. These footpaths are well marked through the forests but care must be taken not to get lost, and a compass and light refreshments are recommended to ensure safety on this route, particularly if walking in the winter. Montrose most likely followed this same route to begin with and then, once past the area where the ski centre now lies and close to Torlundy, he would have turned south, climbing to the lower slopes of Meall an t-Suidhe at 139 730. The only path today that rises towards this height ends at the summit of the pipes system carrying water to the aluminium works below. The evidence from Buchan quoted earlier indicates that Montrose set up camp on the lower slopes of Meall an t-Suidhe, which is point D on the map. Montrose's position, which clearly overlooked Loch Eil, means that he had to be at Creag a'Chail, at 136 744, point E on the map.

Given the flat terrain around Inverlochy, there is no better place to see the climax of Montrose's strategic masterpiece than from the Inverlochy viewpoint at 118 750, point F on the map. There is a lay-by for visitors to park in immediately below the small ridge, and a stile adjacent to the lay-by that allows visitors to cross the fence surrounding the site; note that the steps are oversized and care needs to be taken when climbing over. The ridge is topped with a small stone cairn and metal information board, which serves as the viewpoint, and when standing here the visitor looking east towards Ben Nevis will have the same view as the Covenanters had the morning Montrose's men screamed towards them; it will not be difficult for you to stand there longer than they did, but you will not be facing the wrath of a Highland charge.

Leanachan House, still an isolated and desolate farmstead.

CONCLUSIONS

James Graham, a young, modest and, above all, an honest man, proved that sometimes a person can come along with such self-belief and charisma that they can make the impossible happen just because they believe that they can. Inverlochy is a testament to a man who, faced by forces five times his size, first out-thought them and then got his men to support him in that decision. He then led his ill-equipped and starving army across some of the most inhospitable mountains in the British Isles before descending upon his foes and annihilating them. Inverlochy is one of the shortest battles ever fought; it may have lasted no more than ten minutes, and that is from the time Montrose's men started to charge to when the second Covenanter line broke and ran. Although the battle was short, it was the culmination of a three-day march built solely on grit and determination by an army with little food, poor clothing and through the most atrocious of weather without the modern aids of detailed maps. Inverlochy is a testament to the genius of one man, Montrose.

LOCAL ATTRACTIONS

Inverlochy has a few shops and there is a hotel on the A82, south of the lay-by that the visitor parks in to survey the battle site. Fort William has plenty of parking,

Creag a'Chail, to the hollow in the middle of the mountain Meall an t-Suidhe, where Montrose and his men spent the night before the battle, looking from the ridge at Inverlochy.

which is currently free out of season, and a number of places to eat and stay, as well as a fair shopping centre. There is also a good tourist information office, which can be found at the central square just to the east of the pedestrianised high street. The whole area has a wealth of outdoor activities to pursue, for which the tourist information centre is invaluable. The nearest railway stations are at Fort William, Spean Bridge and Roy Bridge. The tourist information centre is located in Fort William at Cameron Square; telephone: 01397 703781.

West Highland Museum, Cameron Square, Fort William. [Telephone: 01397 702169. Website: www.westhighlandmuseum.org.uk. Contact the museum for opening times. There is an admission charge.] It is located on the same square as the tourist information office and contains an interesting collection of artefacts and general information on Scottish history, as well as brief details about the battles fought in the area.

Nevis Range, Torlundy. [Telephone: 01397 705825. Website: www.nevis range.co.uk. Contact the centre for opening hours. Charges depend on activities pursued.] A winter ski centre and all-year-round activity centre with mountain biking, walking and a gondola ride to Aonach Mor, beside Ben Nevis.

8

Stow-on-the-Wold – 21 March 1646

GLOUCESTERSHIRE – *OS Landranger 163, Cheltenham and Cirencester, Stow-on-the-Wold (187 283)*

Stow-on-the-Wold was to be the last battle of the first English Civil War, and it took place a mile or so west of the Fosse Way, an arterial road in seventeenth-century England. While Charles waited anxiously at Oxford for news of a new army that Sir Jacob Astley was bringing to him, he was negotiating with France, Ireland and even the Pope for military aid to allow him to continue the war against his Parliament. But this new force was a raw army, ill fed and ill clothed, and it faced the unenviable task of trying to march seventy miles across the Midlands, avoiding Parliamentarian garrisons on the way and aware that it was being pursued relentlessly on its march south. As the Parliamentarian troops closed in, the experienced Astley knew that to stand a chance of success, he must beat off his pursuers and gain a breathing space in which to race for Oxford. Accordingly, a mile or so west of Stow, he turned and deployed his men for battle. This really was the very last chance for the King: if Astley failed, then Charles I would have to face the harsh reality that the Civil War was over, and with it the chance of regaining his throne.

PRELUDE TO BATTLE

Following Charles's crushing defeat at Naseby in Northamptonshire on 14 June 1645, the King's cause looked doomed. The Royalists were now desperately short of both men and arms and the situation was made worse by the destruction of his remaining field armies at the battles of Langport in Somerset on 10 July 1645 and Rowton Heath near Chester on 24 September 1645. In Scotland, a brilliant campaign fought by the Marquis of Montrose against overwhelming odds was brought to a crushing end at the battle of Philiphaugh on 13 September 1645. This news, arriving after that of the

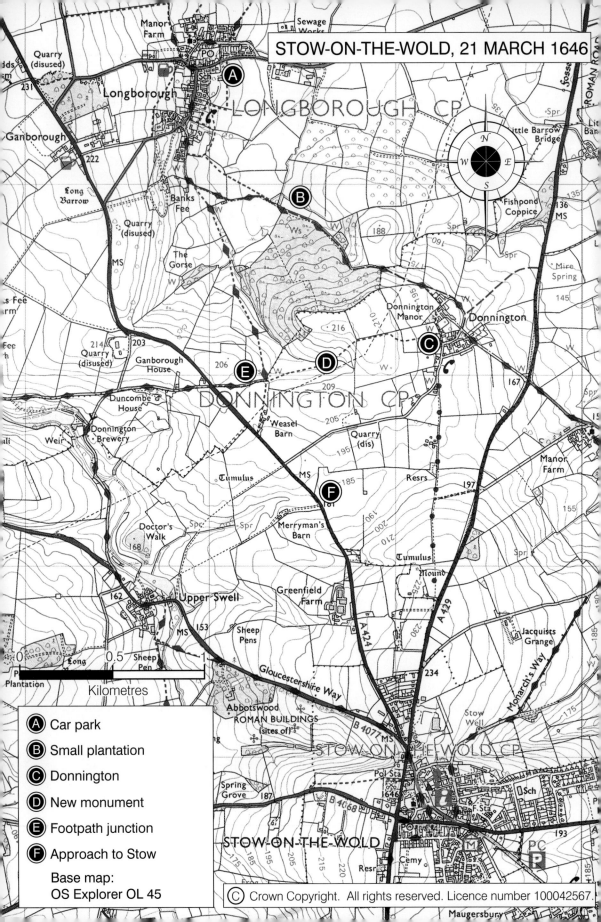

STOW-ON-THE-WOLD, 21 MARCH 1646

Manor Farm
Quarry (disused)
Longborough
Ganborough
222
Long Barrow
Banks Fee
The Gorse
MS
Quarry (disused)
214 203
Quarry (disused)
Ganborough House
Duncombe House
Donnington Brewery
Weir
Tumulus
Doctor's Walk
168
162
Upper Swell
153
Sheep Pens
Greenfield Farm
Sheep Pen
Plantation
Kilometres
0.5
Long

LONGBOROUGH CP
188
216
206
209
205
195
Weasel Barn
Quarry (dis)
MS
Merryman's Barn
185
197
Tumulus
200
210
Resrs
Mound

DONNINGTON CP

Donnington Manor
Donnington
167

Little Barrow Bridge
Fishpond Coppice 136 MS
135
Mire Spring
145

Manor Farm
155

Jacquists Grange

Monarch's Way
234
A 429
A 424

Gloucestershire Way
Abbotswood
ROMAN BUILDINGS (sites of)
Spring Grove 187
B 4068
STOW-ON-THE-WOLD CP
Pol Sta
1646
B 4077 MS
Stow Well
Sch
193
STOW-ON-THE-WOLD
Cemy
Resr
Maugersbury

A Car park
B Small plantation
C Donnington
D New monument
E Footpath junction
F Approach to Stow

Base map:
OS Explorer OL 45

defeat at Rowton Heath, was a bitter blow to Charles. Throughout the winter months of 1645/6, the Parliamentarians, now free from the risk of attack by mobile Royalist forces, began the mopping-up exercise in England, capturing castles and towns that held out loyal to the King to the last. But Charles was a very stubborn man and, still refusing to believe that his cause was lost, he instructed one of his most respected supporters, Sir Jacob Astley, to rally all the men possible from the western Midlands and secure their passage to Oxford. If the King could buy more time with a new army in the field, then this would give him a greater chance of securing foreign aid to assist the defence of his throne. Sir Jacob, a 66-year-old veteran of the wars, had scraped together 3,000 men to form the nucleus of an army from the garrisons of Shropshire, Staffordshire and Worcestershire. Many of these men had not seen action in the field before and were more used to performing garrison duties in towns and castles, possibly miles from any military confrontation.

Stow-on-the-Wold is one of the highest towns in England and was originally a fortified settlement alongside an ancient road, the Roman Fosse Way. In the English Civil War, this road was one of the main routes south and as such was a vital point for an army travelling to Oxford from the west. Astley knew that his enemies would also try to reach the town of Stow-on-the-Wold. As all the approach routes were uphill, it was an excellent place from which to exercise control of the local countryside and any troops that may wish to move through it. It is most likely that Astley's army was following the old salt road to Stow-on-the-Wold, which still exists in part today from Droitwich in Worcestershire, with the Parliamentarians following the same route. As it transpired, Astley and his makeshift army managed to keep ahead of their Parliamentary pursuers, but with each day the doom that was behind them came ever closer and it appears, according to local historian Giles Dickson, that 'all the way from Broadway Hill, there had been a series of running fights against the Royalist rear guard' (author's interview). Astley was an experienced general and he knew that continued attacks on his rear would result in the disintegration of his army, especially given their lack of experience and their poor morale. There was nothing more he could do but stand and fight. It was the night of 20 March when Astley chose to pull his army off the road and head north for the small village of Donnington, to the western side of which was a crescent-shaped ridge. How Astley knew of, or found out about, this ridge is a matter of conjecture, but it was a perfect place to fight a defensive battle.

The interpretive monument at Donnington commemorating the battle of Stow. It is upon this ridge that many musket balls have been found.

RECONSTRUCTING THE BATTLE

Throughout the night of 20 March, Astley's men arrayed themselves on the high ground between the villages of Longborough and Donnington. This was a strong position and one from which determined men could gain a victory if the enemy could be enticed into attacking uphill. The advantage of ground is important, particularly in an army that is nervous, since it leads to an improvement in morale. The enemy has to attack you uphill, while your musketeers can use the higher ground to bring more muskets to bear. If the troops come to hand-to-hand combat, then it is far easier to push down than up, and it takes more courage to advance some way uphill knowing all the time that your opponent has all of the advantages. The Parliamentarians formed their troops on some sloping ground just east of Longborough. It is unclear how many men were under Brereton's command but they certainly outnumbered the Royalists. Roy Field, in his booklet *Stow-on-the-Wold 1646*, calculates that the Parliamentarian army was composed as follows. Colonel Morgan held the centre with at least 2,000 men, mostly infantry but with a few cavalry in support. In addition there was a smaller contingent of Herefordshire men under a

Commander Birch, say an additional 500 men. On the right flank were 800 of Sir William Brereton's men all of whom were horse, though it seems that at least 200 of these were dragoons as opposed to heavy cavalry. A unit of Gloucestershire men on the left flank completed the army; though their number is unknown, an estimate of around 700–800 men would be an informed guess, based on the average size of a regiment when on campaign. These numbers would give a total Parliamentarian force of not less than 4,000 men and a sizeable advantage with which to offset their disadvantage of terrain.

Apparently both sides successfully deployed in the dark and then waited for daybreak to come. It must have been an eerie time that those soldiers passed across the valley from each other, each side waiting to see when their mettle would be tested. The occasional glow of a pipe, or a musketeer's match, must have been all they saw of each other until the first light of dawn brought the darkness and the shadows to life. The Parliamentarians, however, had waited long enough and advanced their whole line towards the waiting Royalists. Roy

A disciplined pike block protects its vulnerable musketeers from marauding cavalry. (Susanne Atkin, Fairfax Battalia)

FLAGS AND COLOURS OF THE CIVIL WAR

Almost from the dawn of military activity, armies and units within those armies have carried flags, banners or symbols to allow recognition among their allies and to provide a morale-boosting rallying point in times of battle. In the Civil War, the flags and standards carried were known as the colours, a name that had originated in the sixteenth century, and they were made from silk taffeta. The cavalry carried small standards just 2ft square, which, if they were regimental, would have some related colour or device common to each troop. Independent troops of horse would have their own slogans, the graffiti of the day, to carry insults to their opponents as they fought, or morale-boosting messages, such as this example from an unknown Royalist standard: 'I will die rather than turn aside'. Interestingly, both sides in the war claimed that God was on their side, one proclaiming 'For God and Parliament', the other 'For God and King'. In addition to a vertical standard carried by the regiment, the cornets would also have a small standard attached to their trumpets. In contrast to plain standards of the infantry, the cavalry standards were fringed.

Infantry colours were 6ft square and had the cross of St George in the upper canton, i.e. nearest the staff. The rest of the flag could be all one colour or sectioned diagonally, or in squares, circles or lines; in fact, there was no recognised format. Each company within a regiment had its own colour. These ran through the ranks, thus colonel, lieutenant-colonel, first captain, second captain, etc. As the rank decreased, so the emblem or device particular to that regiment would increase. Thus, if the emblem for a regiment were a star, then there would be none on the colonel's, one star on the lieutenant-colonel's, two on the first captain's, etc. Similarly, there was no predetermined pattern to the emblems or devices that were used, and indeed sometimes the background colour of the flag depicted the coat colour of the regiment, sometimes it did not. Among the devices used were dogs, circles, roses, diamonds and caltrops, as well as stars. In addition, there could also be personal colours carried, which like the cavalry standards contained mottoes, expressions of loyalty, the family crest and, of course, insults.

The Scottish armies carried the traditional blue and white saltire, or variations on it, for almost all their regiments, though Charles II at the battle of Worcester chose the red rampant lion on gold, the traditional colour of the King of Scotland. In Scotland, too, regiments had their own personal flags with mottoes and devices: Montrose's carried black colours bearing a representation of the severed head of Charles I and the motto *'Deo et Victricibus Armus'*. Scottish cavalry chose much larger standards than their English counterparts, and their saltires were roughly 5ft by 4ft in size, in traditional blue and white. The Scottish cavalry also tended to have more sombre colours than south of the border and they also made more use of heraldic devices.

Field indicates that both armies gave cries of encouragement as they closed together and, true to many a Civil War battle, the Royalists secured the initial advantage and routed the left flank of the Parliamentarians: the Gloucestershire men ran.

The centre, again true to fashion, turned into a stalemate as the armies grappled with one another man-to-man to try and gain the advantage. It was Brereton's combined cavalry and dragoon attack that drove back Astley's left wing, breaking both the infantry and cavalry defending the flank and therefore opening the road to Stow. As Brereton closed in on the Royalist centre, the morale of the army collapsed and they began to flee the field. This gave Morgan the chance to pursue his own retreating Gloucestershire men and rally them in time to return to the fight now that the day was clearly won. The battle was over in a short time, probably no more than thirty minutes, but the bloodshed was far from finished as the jubilant Parliamentarians pursued the now ragged Royalists as they scattered across the fields upwards towards Stow-on-the-Wold.

THE BATTLEFIELD TODAY

The most difficult question to answer is where the battle was actually fought. Whether Sir Jacob Astley had prior knowledge of the ridge at Donnington, sadly there appear to be no records to confirm. But he was an experienced and well-travelled soldier and perhaps, as the Duke of Wellington did with the field of Waterloo, he kept it in his 'back pocket'. If he did not know of its existence, then one must assume that Astley either arrived at the head of his army or had scouts inform him of its location, so that he was aware of it before night fell. This is because all written accounts of this battle state that the armies deployed at night, a difficult thing to achieve in the days of verbal and limited written communication. Therefore many historians have argued that the battle had to be fought on the hilly slopes immediately to the west of Stow-on-the-Wold, which is where the Ordnance Survey currently place the battlefield marker on Landranger sheet 163, and not a mile further out at Donnington. They are able to argue this point for a number of reasons: firstly because they believe that Astley could not have found the ridge at Donnington in the dark and therefore he would just have fallen his troops out either side of the road along which they were advancing as they closed in on the high ground approaching Stow-on-the-Wold. This is still a good defensive position but much nearer to the road, rather than seeking for somewhere away from it in the dark. Secondly, the majority of the casualties were inflicted on these slopes close to the town and also in the

The combined attack by Brereton's cavalry and dragoons pushed back the Royalist left flank across the fields in the centre of the picture.

town square itself. Indeed it is a matter of tradition in the town that Digbeth Street, which runs downhill from the square, ran with Royalist blood (R. Field, 'Stow-on-the-Wold 1646', p. 14). Certainly the market square in the centre of Stow-on-the-Wold is where the majority of Royalists were taken prisoner, and these, perhaps as many as 1,700, were held captive overnight in St Edward's Church. Finally, it is concluded that the routed Royalists could not have run all the way from Donnington to Stow-on-the-Wold without being run down by the Parliamentarian cavalry before they reached the town, because it is one and a half miles from Donnington to Stow-on-the-Wold and most of it uphill.

However, against these strong arguments we must examine Donnington's claim. Firstly, extensive research coupled with tradition has always placed the battle upon the Donnington ridge and it is perfectly possible that Astley had either previous experience or scouted intelligence of the terrain. Secondly, local farmers have found a considerable number of musket balls upon the ridge and indeed the local community at Donnington has got together and funded the construction of their own monument to mark the site where the majority of musket balls have been found. Thirdly, the answer to the question of why the fleeing Royalists had time to make an escape of well over a mile before the

Parliamentarians caught up with them is, the author believes, answered by the sequence of events that took place within the battle itself.

When Brereton succeeded in pushing back Astley's left wing, his own left wing was running from the Royalists; effectively the battle was pivoting on the stalemate in the centre. Therefore, as Brereton turned his cavalry onto the rear of the Royalist line, they broke in panic and started to flee. Seeing the situation, Morgan then left the centre to go and rally his fleeing Gloucestershire men, giving time for the Royalists to commence their flight. As some of Brereton's men were described as 'firelocks' – effectively dragoons advancing on foot – it is only natural to assume that, having achieved their aim of driving off the Royalists from the battle site, they then returned for their horses to pursue them from the comfort of the saddle, rather than struggling on foot. This argument is also borne out by the fact that much of the Royalist cavalry made it through to Oxford with news of the defeat, and although some may have run at the first Parliamentarian attack, it is unlikely that they would have escaped if the Parliamentarian pursuit, particularly from the cavalry, had followed immediately after their successful attack.

Therefore it seems that both arguments may in essence be correct. The battle was fought on the ridge near Donnington, for which the evidence of musket balls upon the site is very strong; but in the aftermath of the battle, once the Parliamentarian troops had regrouped, they came on strongly in pursuit of the fleeing Royalists and succeeded in catching the stragglers on the slopes of the hill just outside Stow-on-the-Wold. There was a great slaughter of these unfortunate men, who were slain as the Parliamentarians continued into the town square and caught up with the rest of the Royalist army and Sir Jacob Astley himself. It seems that the Parliamentarian troops were not content with their bloodletting, or perhaps the remaining Royalists chose to fight rather than to be put to the sword as they attempted to surrender. Either way, the death toll continued to rise among the Royalist troops: in all at least 200 died and there were many wounded, as well as the 1,700 recorded as prisoners.

EXPLORING THE BATTLE SITE

Some of these locations can be explored by car but the main battle site can only be reached on foot. The simplest way to explore the site is to park at Longborough and to complete the whole route on foot. This is a walk of around three miles, but can be increased to five miles if the walker wishes to take in Stow-on-the-Wold as part of the tour. The author would recommend doing the

REGIMENTAL COLOURS IN THE CIVIL WAR

As with the flags, there was no predetermined system for deciding the colours of a regiment. The only organised regiments at the start of the war in 1642 were the London trained bands. These regiments were well organised, with their coat colours matching the background colours of the flags they carried, and thus the Earl of Essex was able to command an army with red, white, blue, green, orange and yellow regiments. However, the other regiments were attired according to the whim of the officer commanding them or the person who provided the money to maintain them, and thus other Parliamentarian regiments wore red, notably those of Robartes, Fairfax, Holles and Montague. But the regiments of Constable, Lord Saye and Sele, Cholmley and Heselrige wore blue; Hampden's, Jones's and Manchester's wore green; Gell's and Merrick's wore grey. Luckily, the regiment of Lord Brookes, from Warwick Castle, wore purple and the Earl of Essex's personal regiment wore orange, so at least these last two stood out from the others.

On the Royalist side it was just as confusing. The King's and the Queen's Lifeguards wore red, but so did the regiments of Apsley, Edward Hopton and Prince Rupert's Firelocks. There were at least seven regiments that wore blue, including Lord Hopton's, Prince Rupert's, Gerard's, Pennyman's and Lunsford's. Those regiments raised by Lord Percy, the Marquess of Newcastle, and Sir Ralph Dutton all wore white. There were at least three yellow regiments, Vavasour's, Paulet's and Talbot's, while green was represented by Northampton's, Tillier's and Broughton's. In addition, there were grey- and black-coated forces. Although a wonderful and colourful sight all of these multicoloured forces must have made, it must surely have been a nightmare for the commanders involved, particularly when on campaign, to try to determine whose troops were where. Surprisingly, there are very few instances reported of regiments getting confused with each other, and similarly no accounts of units suffering from 'friendly fire'.

Troops in the Scottish army were more evenly uniformed than the English regiments. 'Hodden grey', a dirty dull kind of grey, was adopted as the standard coat and breeches colour, which was probably well suited to the harsh life of an army on campaign; one cannot imagine Lord Percy's whitecoats staying white for long on the marches they made in pursuit of the King's cause. The Highlanders, however, had no consistency in their colours; they would simply wear their own personal pattern of plaid, as the clan system had not yet been established. Some might wear the plaid, others trews and a doublet, or trews with the plaid over the top; as much clothing as possible would be an advantage, given the harsh Scottish climate and the marches that both sides undertook. However, one garment which does seem to have been common to all Scots is the 'blue bonnet' that they wore upon their heads, sometimes with a cockade attached.

The formation of the New Model Army in 1645 under Sir Thomas Fairfax at last gave someone, albeit a Parliament that had usurped power, authority to lay down some basic disciplines in the army structure. One of those reforms was the adoption of the red coat as the standard British army uniform, something that would last 250 years, until it was discovered that the red provided their enemies with a bright target when on campaign in colonial countries, and so the khaki replaced the red coat. Red is traditionally an excellent colour to pick for a uniform: it served the Spartan armies of Ancient Greece, the Roman legionnaire and the British infantryman extremely well, not least, it is said, because when a soldier is wounded, the coat does not reveal the fact to the enemy.

Donnington walk and then driving and parking in the centre of Stow-on-the-Wold in order to explore the town. Parking is in the very square where so many Royalists died. There are numerous roads and a small car park at Longborough for visitors to leave their vehicles; this is point A on the map. Head south-east along a footpath known as Monarch's Way, which meanders along, skirting fields and woods until coming uphill to a small plantation; this is point B on the map and probably the extreme right flank of the Royalist army.

Proceed towards Donnington and, on reaching the hamlet, turn right as if to enter the village, then right again, heading due west; this is point C on the map. Walk for several hundred yards along the side of a field, often with horses in it, until you reach a hedge-line and a dipping field ahead of you; this is point D on the map. On the other side of the hedge and a little to the left is the new monument. This is where the majority of musket balls have been found and most probably marks the left wing of the Royalist army upon which Brereton's 'firelocks' would have fired as the cavalry charged uphill, eventually routing Astley's men. Head downhill below the monument and follow the public footpath towards the main road and point E. At this spot, another footpath, the Heart of England Way, crosses the footpath you are on. Turn right here and follow this path north all the way back to Longborough, passing through where the Parliamentarian troops were deployed before the battle, eventually arriving back at point A.

Visitors wishing to visit Stow-on-the-Wold on foot should turn left at the Heart of England Way and then walk alongside the A424 towards Stow-on-the-Wold, but this is a busy main road and it is probably safer to cover this part of

The long hill climbing into Stow-on-the-Wold, up which the routed Royalists were pushed and slain by the victorious Parliamentarians.

the route by vehicle. When approaching Stow-on-the-Wold after point F on the map, the last half-mile is steeply uphill and one can imagine both the pursued Royalists and the chasing Parliamentarians struggling towards Stow-on-the-Wold. From the T-junction where the A424 meets the Fosse Way, now the A429, follow the signs for the town centre and park in the main square. St Edward's Church is on the western side of the square.

CONCLUSIONS

The cause was lost for Charles I before Sir Jacob began his campaign from Shropshire, but the old general obeyed his king's command and attempted to come to his aid. Astley's skill and leadership were an important constant in Charles's military campaigns, and his deployment of the Royalist army at Donnington was an excellent one. With more experienced men he might well have won, but even a victory would only have prolonged the inevitable. Everywhere, people, even some of the Parliamentarian Members of Parliament, were sick of the war, in which it is estimated that at least 250,000 may have died, either in conflict or as a result of the sicknesses, typhoid or plague, that the army carried with it from town to city, from village to port. As Sir Jacob Astley sat upon a drum to await the pleasure of his captors, who at least had the decency to give the aged general a seat, he contemplated his fate and the fate of his king and is reputed to have uttered the following poignant words: 'You have done your work boys and may go play, unless you will fall out among yourselves' (J. Rushworth, *Perfect Passages of every daies intelligence from the Parliament's Army* (7 vols, 1659–1701), vol. 6, p. 140). How right Astley would prove to be: the first war might be over but there was still much blood to be shed, and from the chaos and bickering over who should run the country would emerge the order to execute the King, and the appointment of the single most dictatorial leader this country has ever known – one Oliver Cromwell.

LOCAL ATTRACTIONS

Stow-on-the-Wold is a bustling Cotswold market town and attracts a high number of tourists each year. As a result, there are plenty of places to stay, ranging from hotels, through guest houses to inns, as well as numerous places to eat and a fair selection of local shops, including some antique shops and bookshops. There are also public houses in Longborough and on the A424 at Ganborough, close to Donnington, but Donnington itself has no shop or Inn. Scattered around Stow-on-the-Wold are some of the loveliest villages and towns in England: Burford, Bourton-on-the-Water, Moreton-in-Marsh, Chipping Norton, the Swells and the Slaughters are all worth visiting. Each has its own beauty and there are many panoramic walks to be enjoyed. The nearest railway station is at Moreton-in-Marsh. The tourist information centre is located at Hollis House, the Square, Stow-on-the-Wold; telephone: 01451 831082.

Chastleton House near Stow-on-the-Wold. [Telephone: 01608 674355. Website: www.nationaltrust.org.uk. Not open all the year round. Contact the house for opening times and in some cases to book a space for a timed visit. There is an admission charge.] One of England's finest Jacobean houses, having been occupied for over 400 years by the same family, with a wealth of original furniture and fabrics.

9

Killiecrankie – 27 July 1689

PERTH AND KINROSS – *OS Landranger 43, Braemar and Blair Atholl (907 637)*

In Britain the 1680s were a time of bloodshed, rebellion and political transition. In 1688, through the 'Glorious Revolution' (because no blood had been shed), the monarchy of the United Kingdom had changed from a resurgent Catholic James II to a Protestant William of Orange. Yet in the process the peers of England isolated the Stuart monarchy and its heirs and provided the Catholic countries of Europe with a needle with which they would prick England at every opportunity. It also started a romance between the men of the Highlands and the Stuarts, which would continue unabated from revolt to rising for a further sixty years, and that romance would only end with the complete destruction of the Highland way of life. The first of these Jacobite risings placed their army of Highlanders against a Government army of regular troops above the Pass of Killiecrankie, just south of Blair Atholl in the lower highlands of Scotland. Although outnumbered by more than two to one, the Jacobite commander, Viscount Dundee, was confident of destroying the Government force and beginning the quest to put James II back on his rightful throne.

PRELUDE TO BATTLE

Sedgemoor had been fought in 1685 and James II's army had been successful in putting down the Duke of Monmouth's rebellion; Monmouth's claim to the throne was removed along with his head. The reprisals that followed, known as the infamous 'Bloody Assizes' and led by the merciless Judge Jeffreys, resulted in the arrest and trial of 1,500 people. The lucky ones were sold into bonded slavery, destined for Barbados; the majority, though, were hanged. The execution of over a thousand peasants was designed to put fear into the hearts of other subjects, be they noble or pauper, considering rebellion against the King. James II was so encouraged by his success at Sedgemoor that he believed he was the undisputed

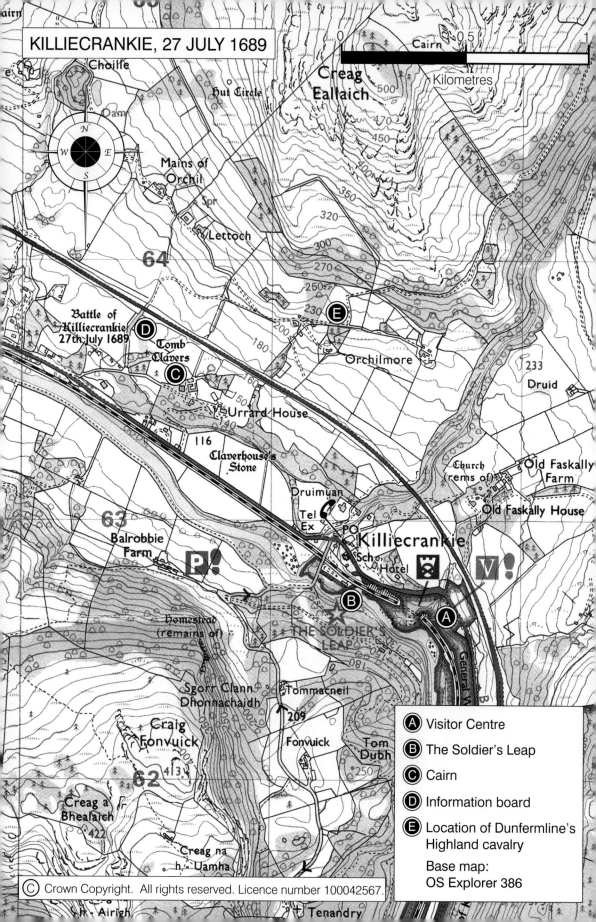

KILLIECRANKIE, 27 JULY 1689

Creag Eallaich

Cairn

500
470
450
400
350
320
300
270
250
230
200
180
160
50
140
116

Choille

Hut Circle

Dam

Mains of Orchil

Spr

Lettoch

64

Battle of Killiecrankie 27th July 1689

Ⓓ

Ⓒ Tomb Clavers

Ⓔ

Orchilmore

233

Druid

Urrard House

Claverhouse's Stone

Druimyan

Tel Ex

PO

Sch.

Hotel

Church (rems of)

Old Faskally Farm

Old Faskally House

63

Balrobbie Farm

Ⓟ !

Ⓥ !

Ⓧ

Killiecrankie

Ⓑ

THE SOLDIER'S LEAP

Ⓐ

General W

Homestead (remains of)

Sgorr Clann Dhonnachaidh

Tommacneil

209

Fonvuick

Tom Dubh

250

Craig Fonvuick

413

62

Creag a Bhealaich

422

Creag na h-Uamha

Tenandry

h. Airigh

Ⓐ Visitor Centre

Ⓑ The Soldier's Leap

Ⓒ Cairn

Ⓓ Information board

Ⓔ Location of Dunfermline's Highland cavalry

Base map: OS Explorer 386

master of his realm and so he decided to press on with his own dispensation of power. Penal laws could be set aside if he chose, Parliament could be dismissed if its views were not in line with his own and, above all, some, if not all, of the Roman Catholic practices could be restored to the English Church.

These extreme measures, following on so soon after the retribution that had been meted out by the army of James II after Sedgemoor, turned the people against their king. So it was that a number of leading statesmen invited William of Orange (James's son-in-law) to come to England to secure his wife's right to the throne; William landed in England on 5 November 1688. James II now began undoing those policies that he had begun to implement, but it was too late. His army deserted him, his followers, who had been dismissed as 'evil' counsellors, were gone, and effectively he was alone save for a few loyal friends. James had already sent his wife and his young son and heir abroad to France; it was now James's turn to flee.

James II's flight from London was nothing short of farcical and it began in disguise on 11 December from Whitehall. James had only got as far as Faversham before he was seized and brought back to London. After a few days, he was taken and imprisoned in Rochester, but was 'allowed' to escape to France, where he was reunited with his wife and son. It was deemed safer to let James flee quietly abroad than to risk turning him into a martyr, which might inflame the fickle population. In France, he was soon introduced to King Louis XIV, who sympathised with his cause and assisted James with troops for his expedition to Ireland a year later. In supporting James in his attempt to regain his throne, Louis was hitting the English from the rear, causing them to move ships and troops away from other regions of the world, so allowing the French more leeway in their movements to expand their empire. Louis saw James as a sound military investment.

In early 1689 James landed in Ireland and on 16 April 1689, Viscount Dundee, known as 'Bonnie Dundee' to his friends, raised James's standard upon Law Hill in Dundee. With him there were just fifty men, though letters were on the way from Ireland stating that James would be sending Irish troops to support the rising in Scotland. The recruitment of followers to Dundee's cause proved very difficult, but William of Orange had not been idle. Hearing of Dundee's arrival in Scotland he ordered the Scottish Convention (the Scottish Parliament, which had unanimously approved William of Orange's appointment on 24 April 1689) to send Major-General Hugh Mackay of Scourie to intercept and destroy Dundee's rebellion.

The news that Mackay was marching against Dundee galvanised some of the clans into action. Support now came from the Catholic clans and the

Scottish Highlands, and eventually 300 Irish troops arrived at Kintyre. The geographical structure of the Highlands, with high mountains split by narrow river valleys, limited the routes by which armies could travel efficiently. Accordingly, intelligence on what the enemy's movements were, or plans might be, was crucial. Armed with that knowledge, someone with a sound understanding of the terrain had a great strategic advantage over his opponent.

Making his way from the Highlands, Dundee made for Blair Castle, or Blair Atholl as it is better known, the home of the Atholl family since 1269. This was a vital strongpoint as it guarded the main route north through the central highlands of Scotland from Perth, via Pitlochry and Kingussie to Inverness. At Blair Castle, the Marquis of Atholl was playing the time-honoured game of 'wait and see who wins' before he committed himself to one side or the other, but there was nothing he could do to prevent Dundee's men from securing the castle. Through intelligence, Dundee knew that Mackay, who had been fruitlessly pursuing Dundee for three months, was now at Perth with an army of regulars.

The majority of Dundee's army were Highlanders and they were eager to march on Mackay's force as soon as possible; they fretted and became frustrated at their inability to close with an enemy that was now but two days away. To Dundee's credit he managed to keep the clan leaders happy by informing them that they would get their chance at Mackay's men as soon as possible. Dundee managed to convince them that to be able to use their famous charge to good effect, the battle had to be fought on ground suitable for such a charge, and the narrow valley of the River Garry below Pitlochry was not the place to fight: the terrain meant that only guerrilla tactics would work on such steep and rough mountain slopes. It was clear that the only place suitable for such a charge was the sloping ground to the north-east of Killiecrankie and that Mackay would have to be given uninterrupted passage to draw his army out into the open, from the narrow confines of the river valley.

Having met his clans, Dundee realised that any kind of defensive, drawing, feint or other subtle manoeuvre was out of the question: once released, the wave of the Highland charge would either envelope the enemy or break upon it. There was no middle way. He also knew that Mackay would make for Blair Castle next. It was the obvious choice, an important stronghold on the main road north, so Mackay had to come through the Pass of Killiecrankie. Once he had laid his plans, Dundee sent the majority of his force north-east from Blair Castle in a circulatory clockwise march that would bring them on to the lower

A white lorry runs along the A9 road indicating where Mackay's Government troops would have stood while Dundee and the Jacobites watched from the heights above.

slopes of Creag Eallaich, and many hundreds of feet above the road below them. He had few cavalry in his army but he sent them on a separate march away from the rest of his army, in order to draw Mackay's attention away from the mountains to his right as he emerged from the Pass of Killiecrankie. Accordingly, the first sighting Mackay's scouts had of the Jacobite forces was a small unit of cavalry coming towards them from the direction of Strathgarry and Blair Castle. Mackay was probably convinced that these horsemen were Dundee's own skirmish patrols out looking for the Government army. He took the bait and followed.

Too late, Mackay realised his predicament when he saw the clans marching up onto the high ground to his right. Retreat for Mackay's men was impossible because the Jacobites would soon be no more than a musket shot away, so if the Williamites tried to turn and run, then a Highland charge would catch them deploying and they would be crushed. Mackay had no choice but to deploy on the ground that Dundee had chosen for him. He therefore sent his men up the first slope of the hill, to the right of the narrow road that had been their path for the fifteen miles from Dunkeld, and they began to deploy in the face of the Highlanders above.

THE JACOBITE REBELLIONS

The Latin form of James is Jacobus and following James II's self-inflicted exile in France, his supporters in Britain became known as 'Jacobites'. The two most famous Jacobite Rebellions were in 1715 and 1745. But there were a whole series of rebellions that began within a year of James II abandoning his crown. In all, there were six attempted Jacobite risings and they occurred in 1689, 1708, 1715, 1719, 1744 and 1745. In every case, the Jacobites believed that when they arrived in Scotland, mass support would appear, and then when they marched into England even more people would rush to join their army for the triumphal march into London. France and Spain were only too glad to give money, lend ships and sometimes even send troops into Scotland to assist the Jacobite cause, because it gave Britain a war on two fronts, tying down at home troops and ships that Britain would have preferred to use abroad.

The Jacobite rebellions should not been seen as a war between England and Scotland. It was very much a civil war, with Highland Scots fighting Lowland Scots, with Catholic against Protestant, rich against poor, and clan against clan. Although it was a series of civil wars fought largely in Scotland, troops from Holland, England, Wales, Ireland, France, Spain and Germany would all take part. The French and Spanish spent in today's terms millions of pounds attempting to restore the Stuart monarchy and thousands of French and Spanish troops drowned as their ships were harried to destruction time and again either by the Royal Navy or the storms that seem to have come to the aid of the British Isles on more than one occasion.

The most famous rebellion was 'the '45', which saw Bonnie Prince Charlie arrive with just seven comrades in the Outer Hebrides on 2 August 1745. Slowly the rebellion gained momentum until at Prestonpans on 21 September Lord George Murray commanding the Jacobite army routed the Government army of Sir John Cope. The way to England was open and after much debate the advance across the border was undertaken, but by then it was 3 November. The 6,000-strong Jacobite army reached Derby, before their morale finally wilted on 4 December and the retreat to Scotland began. To meet this serious rebellion, regular troops were recalled from the continent where the War of the Austrian Succession raged, and the Duke of Cumberland led the Government forces. Despite their predicament the Jacobites succeeded in routing the Government troops at Clifton Moor on 18 December and then Falkirk on 17 January, each time using the terrain and Highland charge to maximum effect. Eventually the two armies met on Culloden Moor on 16 April 1746. Charles, the inexperienced, dogmatic heir to the throne, chose terrain totally unsuitable to the Highland style of fighting and must be seen as responsible for the disaster that ensued. The

Government troops won the battle and their reprisals, as they hunted the fugitives across the land, ensured that there would never be another Jacobite rising. The price that the Highlanders paid for sixty years of loyalty to the Stuart cause was to have their traditional way of life destroyed forever as over the next sixty years they fell victim to the 'Highland Clearances'.

RECONSTRUCTING THE BATTLE

The Government army of this period was organised in line with contemporary military practice, armed with the latest military hardware, and it would thus have been recognisable across the majority of western Europe. The army consisted of regular troops dressed in regimental uniforms to laid-down colours and armed with either the matchlock or the new flintlock musket. Each musketeer also carried the plug bayonet, the innovation that allowed him to turn his musket into an offensive mêlée weapon. This was responsible for reducing the number of pikemen within a regiment to a mere handful, if there were any present at all. The army also had regular cavalry, normally dragoons armed with sword, pistols and a musket, and a small unit of elite cavalry, either horse guards or horse grenadiers. There would also be a number of small cannon, light guns able to move with the army across the appalling roads of the Highlands. These regular infantry were trained to fire steady volleys into the approaching enemy, the theory being that the devastation caused by these volleys would destroy the enemy's morale as well as their numbers, and ensure that any charge did not make it into contact. The artillery would fire in support of the infantry by concentrating on the densest or most sensitive targets available.

The cavalry would be used either to exploit a weakness in the enemy by advancing to complete the rout of a faltering enemy unit or to steady an allied regiment by advancing in support of the infantry engaged. In sharp contrast to this, and as an exception to the other armies of western Europe, the Scots who formed the ranks of the Jacobite armies were still attired and armed in exactly the same way as when they first came to prominence a hundred years earlier. The clansmen would be alike in terms of appearance and in the weapons they carried, but each would be different in that there was no uniformity in the supply of their weapons or the source of their clothing. The Highlander in theory carried a musket, a sword, a shield and up to two pistols. Some chose to carry the two-handed sword, the claymore, instead of the more common broadsword, while others preferred another ancient weapon, the two-handed

Lochaber-axe. Not all Highlanders carried muskets, and so those men who had them tended to form the front ranks of the regiments. They were dressed in traditional clothing of shirt and doublet, with either trews or the traditional plaid, serving as both cloak and kilt.

On p. 20 of his book *Memoirs of the Lord Viscount Dundee, The Highland Clans*, published by F.E. Robinson and Company in 1903, Henry Jenner gives a clear picture of how the Highlanders reacted once given the order for the advance: they discarded their 'plads, haversacks, and all other utensils, and marched resolutely and deliberately in their shirts and doublets, with their fusils [muskets], swords, targets, and pistols ready'. The Highland charge was, by all accounts, a fearsome sight to behold; it began, as Henry Jenner describes, with the discarding of all surplus kit, which was simply left where it fell. The charge would then gain momentum until the Highlanders were within a few seconds of hitting the enemy, at which point they would fire their muskets to cause as much confusion as possible before the charge made contact. Once fired, the muskets were dropped to the ground and the pistols were then drawn to fire into the face of the enemy, before these too were thrown aside. Finally, at the last second, the Highlander would draw either the claymore or the broadsword and bring it crashing down onto the head, or across the face, of the man before him. It took a brave man to withstand such an assault and the history of the Jacobite uprisings shows that, in the majority of battles, the Government troops had no stomach to stand and face such a brutal assault.

Mackay knew that his position was precarious. The enemy were some 400ft above him on sloping ground and to his rear were the treacherous banks of the River Garry, with no escape route should his army be worsted. Yet Mackay did have some advantages: his army was twice the size of Dundee's, and his men were regulars trained in disciplined firing, which meant that they should easily be able to fire two or three volleys per minute. As Mackay's men deployed, he encouraged them with these facts and assured them that if they stood firm, their volleys would win the day. Mackay knew that the terrain was such that once his force was deployed there would be no room to manoeuvre, and so he decided to risk having no reserve so as to be able to bring all his available firepower to bear on the enemy. To achieve this, Mackay dispensed with a second line of foot troops and instead he placed his two units of cavalry to act as a reserve behind the centre of his infantry. He also placed a few infantry in Urrard House, presumably because this would be a rallying point if his troops buckled from the Highlanders' assault. Mackay also feared being outflanked, especially towards the narrow Killiecrankie pass through which his army had just

Urrard House in the left centre of the picture marks the centre of the Government position.

marched. If his army was defeated and they were cut off from that passage out of the Highlands, Mackay knew that none of them would escape. Hence, to ensure that he could not be outflanked, Mackay extended his line, which meant that once his army was deployed it was only three ranks deep, a very thin red line.

Dundee knew that to stand a chance of victory his men had to break the Government troops with their first charge. Having seen the deployment below him, Dundee arranged his troops in columns by clan. So instead of charging downhill in a drawn-out line, giving all of Mackay's infantry a target straight ahead of them, seven densely packed columns would charge, aiming to hit certain Government regiments ahead of them, but risking flanking fire from those Government regiments not engaged. This was a risky strategy, but Dundee gambled that the flanking regiments would not have time to manoeuvre into position before the Highland charge was past them, and their fire would be useless unless they would risk firing into a mêlée which involved more of their own troops than their enemy's.

Mackay's army numbered 4,600 foot and around 500 horse and consisted of Lowland Scots and Dutch troops arranged just to the east of Urrard House, with that building close to the centre of his line and the most likely place that the reserve of cavalry was deployed. Going to the left of Urrard House were the regiments of Kenmure, Ramsay and Balfour, with between 650 and 750 men in each, with a small unit of Lauder's Fusiliers, no more than 200 strong, on the extreme left flank. To the front of Urrard House were the two regiments of cavalry, each approximately 250 strong under the command of Annandale and Benhaven. To the right of the cavalry, and arced towards the Highlanders so as not to be outflanked at the entrance to Killiecrankie pass, were the regiments of Leven and Hastings, each with 850 men in number. Between the regiments of Leven and Hastings, Mackay placed his own regiment, a further 650 men. Dundee had only a little over 2,000 men. As Mackay looked up the hill of Creag Eallaich above him, he would have seen seven Highland clan units deployed from left to right as follows: Macleans, 200 men; the Irish regiment, 400 men; Clanranald, 600 men; Glengarry, 300 men; the Earl of Dunfermline's horse no more than 50 men; Camerons, 240 men; and finally the Sleat Macdonalds, 300 men. This meant that, when the charge came, Dundee would be throwing 1,400 men on his right against the 2,250 men on Mackay's left, while the 2,350 men on Mackay's right would be receiving an attack from Dundee's left of just 540 men.

It seems that all the deployment was completed by early afternoon, and then the psychological warfare began. Dundee was determined that his small army would not strike until the time was right. It was high summer; the sun was behind Mackay's men and into the faces of the Jacobites, and Dundee was prepared to wait for it to dip behind the mountains across the valley to the west, so that his men would have a clear view when they charged. Dundee also knew that the Government troops had been marching for some weeks in pursuit of his Jacobite force. They had arrived in the morning after another long march from Perth, then they had deployed, and now they were standing at the ready, waiting for the Jacobite advance to begin. Therefore, the longer they were kept on their feet, the more fatigued they would become and the less attentive they would be. If Dundee could restrain the clans for the rest of the sunny afternoon, the regulars would be at their weakest in early evening. To increase the pressure on their intended victims, the Highlanders started their howls, intimidating, eerie calls that made the blood run cold to hear it. For hours the Highlanders bayed, ignoring the musket and intermittent cannon shots that Mackay sent into their ranks to try and compel them into charging; but Dundee was still prepared to wait, and this control of the clans clearly demonstrates his tremendous leadership.

At about eight o'clock in the evening Dundee gave the order to advance. With each clan having a nominated Government regiment to assault, the 2,000 men began their charge. Although they were accustomed to such terrain, it cannot have been easy for the Highlanders to move rapidly over the sloping

A ferocious Highland charge performed by a re-enactment group conveys something of the terror that these charges instilled into the nervous Government regiments. *(Geoff Buxton)*

rough ground, especially as their momentum gathered with the advance. Mackay had seen the ground before his men as a killing field, and at approximately 80yd his men let forth a tremendous volley. Mackay had been proved right, for as many as 700 Highlanders fell to the floor. One-third of their force was gone, but the remainder poured on and the charge was more than Mackay's men could bear. The Jacobites fired their running volley at about 50yd from the Government troops before drawing their swords and crashing, pistols firing, blades swirling, into the line.

The Government troops on the left had failed to reload and fire a second volley into the closing Jacobites; and then they struggled to fix their plug bayonets into position and so had to fend off their opponents with their basic muskets. Their end was swift: the Government troops on the left of Urrard House all broke into rout. Mackay, seeing that his right regiments were still intact, called for his cavalry to assault the Jacobite units ahead of him to stabilise the situation, but as he rode forward he turned and looked behind him to find that only one sergeant had followed him, and the rest of his cavalry turned and fled as Mackay's routed infantry ran through them. Mackay, by a miracle, passed unscathed through the Highlanders' ranks and ended up higher up the hill, alone on the heather, looking down on his army's destruction. At this crucial moment in the battle, Dundee himself had led his own cavalry regiment down the hill, and he saw Dunfermline go on and capture the Government cannon; but then another steady volley of musket fire from Mackay's own regiment hit the Jacobite general, and Dundee fell, mortally wounded, to the ground.

The battle was effectively over in less than twenty minutes. Mackay eventually arrived back at Stirling with less than 500 men. It is estimated that at least 2,000 died on the field, with 500 more killed in the pursuit and the remaining 2,000 scattered to who knows what end. Some indication of the brutality of that few minutes of hand-to-hand fighting is illustrated by a quote from an eyewitness of the battle, Sir Ewen Cameron of Lochiel, who says in the work *Memoirs of Sir Ewen Cameron of Lochiel, Chief of the Clan Cameron* ed. John Drummond (Edinburgh, The Abbotsford Club, 1842), 'When day returned, the Highlanders went and took a view of the field of battle, where the dreadful efforts of their fury appeared in many horrible figures. The enemy lay in heaps almost in the order they were posted; but so disfigured with wounds, and so hashed and mangled, that even the victors could not look upon the amazing proofs of their own ability and strength without surprise and horror. Many had their heads divided into two halves by one blow, others had their sculls cutt-off above the eares by a back-strock.'

After Killiecrankie, Colonel Cannon, leader of the small Irish regiment, took command of the Jacobite forces. First, the Highlanders returned to Blair Castle with Bonnie Dundee's body for burial. Having regrouped and seen their ranks swell to around 5,000, the Highlanders began another march south, through Killiecrankie pass and on towards Perth. They arrived at Dunkeld to find that the newly raised Earl of Angus's regiment had fortified the town against the approaching Jacobites. Cannon was already having trouble keeping the minds of his clans on the job at hand, for he did not have the diplomacy or tenacity of Dundee. On 21 August the Jacobites began an assault on the town that lasted for several hours, but they inflicted few casualties on the Government troops and suffered several hundred themselves. The Jacobite tactics were suited to open assaults, not sieges or street fighting. Accordingly, having been worsted, the Highlanders returned north to Blair Castle before drifting back to their homes in the mountains. Cannon and his Irish troops wintered at Lochaber and attempted to raise the rebellion again in 1690, but on 1 May at Cromdale they were defeated and the 1689 rising was over.

THE BATTLEFIELD TODAY

The nature of the terrain means that in essence the battlefield has changed little over the last 300 years, save for the expansion of housing and farm buildings that have been constructed around Killiecrankie village and Urrard House. It is still possible to access the lower slopes of Creag Eallaich and view the battle site from Dundee's initial position on the hills above. The memorial cairn to the clan dead can also be seen, as can the spot where it is believed that many of the Government officers were buried. Much of the land is farmed, and consists of rough pasture with sheep and cattle grazing the enclosed fields. The principal blot on the landscape is the main trunk road from the A9. This road runs right through the heart of the battle site; in fact the verge of the left-hand carriageway when heading north (that nearest to the River Garry) most probably marks the front line of Mackay's regiments. Unlike other battles, the location of the battle site is not hard to determine: Urrard House serves as an excellent central point for the location of Mackay's troops and this allows the deduction of the slopes down which Dundee's troops charged when assaulting Mackay's army.

The cairn to the fallen of the battle of Killiecrankie, which stands in the grounds of Urrard House, can only be reached along the designated pathway.

CHANGES IN WARFARE

In warfare as well as politics the late seventeenth century was a period of transition. Regiments of troops in the English Civil Wars were formed of two types of infantrymen, or foot: the musketeer and the pikeman. The role of the pikeman was to protect the slow-firing musketeers from marauding cavalry, giving the musketeers time to reload and fire. When each side had softened the other up with a volley or two of musketry, the regiment would advance, with the pikemen going forward to deliver the final charge.

At the outset of the English Civil War, the ratio of pike to musket was supposed to be 1:2. In reality and certainly in the Royalist armies it was at least 3:1 in favour of the pike. By the end of the war nearly all the Royalist foot regiments consisted of men who were solely armed with muskets, preferring to fire and then charge using their musket butts as the offensive weapon. The New Model Army, however, was reformed under Thomas Fairfax along traditional lines, with one pikeman to every two musketeers. This ratio of the number of pikemen to musketeers was mirrored across the whole of western Europe as military ideas became copied from one country to another.

However, by 1670 a new invention began to creep into all of the western European armies. According to historical tradition, sometime around 1610 at Bayonne in France, a short, sharp-edged and pointed weapon was designed for attaching to the muzzle of a musket, and it was called a bayonet. The idea was that the musketeer could insert the bayonet into the muzzle of his own musket and turn his firearm into a short pike, an attacking mêlée weapon, and so after his volleys of musketry the musketeer could deliver his own *coup de grâce*. This early design of bayonet was referred to as a 'plug' bayonet because it fitted into the mouth of the musket barrel. The drawback of this new weapon was that it prevented the musket from being fired, which meant that if you were not quick enough with your last volley and fitting your bayonet, it was possible for a charging enemy to hit you before you were ready – with disastrous results.

The most important development came in 1688 when Sébastian le Prestre de Vauban invented the socket or 'sock' bayonet. His bayonet slipped over the mouth of the musket barrel, and slid down the outside of the barrel before being twisted and locked into a small but strong fixing, which held the bayonet in place until the musketeer wanted to remove it. This innovation meant two things, firstly that the bayonet was solidly fixed to the musket and would not dislodge in hand-to-hand combat, thus giving the musketeer greater confidence in its fighting ability. Secondly, because the barrel was not blocked, the musketeer could carry on firing until the last possible moment before receiving the enemy's charge. This design of socket bayonet would remain basically unchanged for the next 250 years and would be used across the world, notably by the massed armies of the Napoleonic Wars, where the red-coated British infantry would become synonymous with great firepower and a thin red line of steel.

EXPLORING THE BATTLE SITE

Killiecrankie is well served with a display board situated on the battlefield and a visitor centre. Unfortunately the visitor centre is at the north end of the Killiecrankie pass about half a mile short of the actual battlefield. If approaching from the north-east, the direction from which Dundee reached the battle, then it is best to commence with a visit to Blair Castle and then move south. If approaching from the south via Pitlochry, which is the way Mackay came, then it is best to start with the visitor centre and the Soldier's Leap and then move north. I shall assume an approach from the south. The visitor centre is situated on the B8079 and it is important for visitors to the site to take one of the relevant exits off the A9, which are some distance from Killiecrankie village. The visitor centre was refurbished over the winter of 2004/5 and provides a wealth of additional information on this battle and the Jacobite period of history. This is point A on the map.

From the visitor centre a well-signposted path leads to the Soldier's Leap, point B on the map. It was at this point immediately following the battle that one of the Government soldiers, Donald MacBean, found himself pursued by three screaming Jacobites intent on his execution. Being cornered by his descent towards the raging torrent of the Garry he was faced with the dilemma of either turning to face his would-be assassins, or attempting to leap the river, at its narrowest point some 18ft wide. In desperation, MacBean leapt literally for his life and amazingly landed safely on the other side. Since this date, the location has been known as 'Soldier's Leap'. This incident also confirms the fact that the Jacobites discarded their firearms in the charge, and did not return for them until a considerable time after the battle; otherwise the pursuers, seeing what their fugitive was about to do, would have surely loaded and fired their muskets or pistols at the fleeing redcoat.

After exploring these adjacent sites the visitor should proceed along the B8079 until passing the end of Killiecrankie village; then a road sign warning of a 'blind summit' should be looked for, after which there is a right turn which doubles back on itself. This is a minor road, which, after a few hundred yards, forks: straight on to Urrard House, and left towards the hills. Having taken the left turn, the visitor should look into the wooded field to the right. Here the memorial cairn to the fallen stands in the centre of a boggy wood; this is point C on the map. A little further on, a small bridge which takes the minor road underneath the A9 will be seen ahead. Just before this on the right is a pull-in by a large gate, which is the entrance to the site of the information board; this is

The boiling waters of the River Garry across which redcoat Donald MacBean leapt 18ft to save his life from his Jacobite pursuers.

point D on the map. The visitor should park in this space and from here can return on foot to visit the cairn in the wooded field below. Please note that this land is a private working farm and is part of the Urrard House estate.

There is an access path to and from the cairn, and given the boggy nature of the ground it is advisable for safety reasons to keep to the path. Having visited the two memorials, proceed under the A9 and follow the road which slowly deteriorates as it reaches the two farms which are on the lower slopes of Creag Eallaich. There are several places to stop and turn round, but care needs to be taken as the land is not all enclosed and Highland cattle and sheep wander freely. This is a 'no through road' and when you are coming to the end you are where the Jacobites rested and waited for Mackay's men to tire in the July sun below them.

Point E on the map marks the approximate location of Dunfermline's Highland cavalry at the centre of the Jacobite army and the point from which Dundee would have made his advance. Standing and watching the traffic moving on the A9 below, the visitor will appreciate how far the sound travels; it takes little imagination to realise how dreadful the mournful howls of the

Highlanders must have sounded to the Government troops below. This wonderful viewpoint is the place from where the Jacobites would have started their charge, and it is an excellent place from which to survey the battle site, but as yet there are no information boards to explain the dispositions to visitors. However, taking the far side of the A9 to represent the Government front line will give some idea as to the width of the deployment, and Urrard House, among the trees behind, marks the centre of the army and was roughly the position of the Government cavalry reserve. Having stood and pondered the battle site, the visitor must retrace the journey back to the B8079. It is possible to leave vehicles at the visitor centre or Blair Atholl and explore all of the locations mentioned on foot, though it would require a full day's walk.

CONCLUSIONS

Had Dundee not been killed, it is most likely that even more than the 5,000 Highlanders that assembled at Blair Castle after Killiecrankie would have risen in support of the Jacobites. Any rebellion, as Kett's clearly demonstrates, relies on the strength, belief and charisma of its leadership. In Dundee, the Jacobites had a natural, intelligent commander with the support and understanding of his men, and Cannon, who was to succeed Dundee, was just not of the same calibre. If any rising was going to succeed in putting a Stuart heir back on the British throne it had to be done at a time when Britain was weak, when the idea was fresh and when maximum support could be gained from France and Spain; the first few years of William's reign was the perfect time to strike. Alas for James II, the greatest chance he had of regaining his throne was first won and then lost in the same evening as the valiant Bonnie Dundee fell on the sloping field of the incredible victory of Killiecrankie.

LOCAL ATTRACTIONS

Pitlochry is the nearest town to Killiecrankie and can offer an excellent range of hotels, guesthouses, restaurants and inns. There is also a good selection of shops and places to obtain food. The nearest railway stations are at Pitlochry and Blair Atholl. The tourist information centre is located at 22 Atholl Road, Pitlochry; telephone: 01796 472215/472751.

Blair Castle, Blair Atholl. [Telephone: 01796 481207. Website: www.blair-castle.co.uk. Opening hours are seasonal. An admission charge applies.] This is the location of Dundee's assembly before the battle of Killiecrankie and his resting place after his death. A fantastic building and well worth visiting.

Pitlochry Salmon Ladder. [Telephone: 01796 473152. No website. Opening hours are seasonal. An admission charge applies.] This simple but effective artificial watercourse is maintained by Scottish and Southern Energy. There is a visitor centre and an exhibition where people can learn about salmon and see the fish as they migrate upriver through the hydro-electricity plant via a purpose-built ladder.

Killiecrankie Visitor Centre. [Telephone: 01796 473233. Website: www.nts.org.uk. Opening hours are seasonal, so contact the centre before visiting. An admission charge applies.] Located half a mile south of the battle, this centre has been refurbished in 2005. Walks from here take the visitor to the Soldier's Leap.

10

Goudhurst – 21 April 1747

ROYAL TUNBRIDGE WELLS, KENT – *OS Landranger 188, Maidstone and Royal Tunbridge Wells (723 377)*

Goudhurst is a small village situated high on the Kent Weald, in an area of rolling hills which are bisected by numerous valleys, many with small streams and rivers. The Weald has changed little during the last 500 years, and is predominantly an agricultural area, part of the 'Garden of England', as Kent is often termed. Situated almost midway between London and the south coast, Goudhurst was just one of a series of villages that became associated with the great smuggling gangs of the eighteenth century. Importantly, Goudhurst is unique among British battles. It is the story of a band of bullied Englishmen fed up with the lawlessness of the time, who, with no support from the authorities, decided to take the law into their own hands and confront a gang of ruthless and sadistic smugglers, the Hawkhurst Gang. This was a battle in which no regular troops were involved and in which the action that ensued can only be likened to an English equivalent of a 'Wild West shoot-out'.

PRELUDE TO BATTLE

On the Kentish Weald, smuggling seems to have begun in earnest around 1710, when a Gabriel Tomkins, a bricklayer from Tunbridge Wells, became leader of a group of wool smugglers that became known as the Mayfield Gang. This gang were by all accounts non-violent: they would tie up any who crossed them, but release them later. These 'owlers' (a Kentish generic term for wool smugglers) had a simple trade going: they shipped wool from their own farms to France and returned with brandy and silk. Some of the inns between Tunbridge Wells and the coast bear the name the 'Woolpack' and these, according to local legend, were 'safe houses' where wool could be stored en route to the coast. The Mayfield Gang mostly consisted of farmers and their labourers and they all lived and worked in a

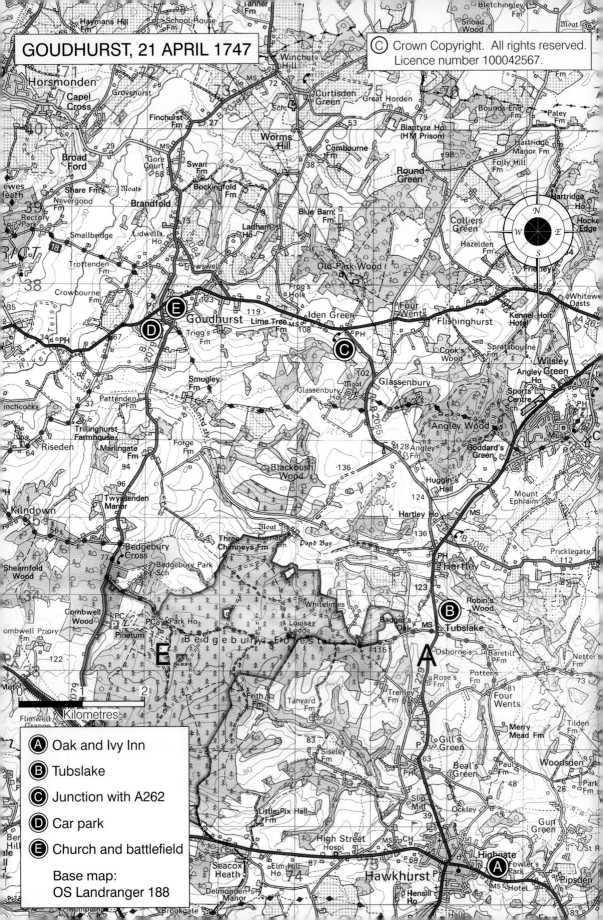

GOUDHURST, 21 APRIL 1747

Kilometres

A Oak and Ivy Inn

B Tubslake

C Junction with A262

D Car park

E Church and battlefield

Base map:
OS Landranger 188

triangle formed by the settlements of Seaford, Hastings and Tunbridge Wells. This gave the gang a length of coast of almost twenty-five miles and a variety of beaches from which to operate. Owing to their non-violent approach and their generosity in spending their profits within the local community, the Mayfield Gang were well supported by the local population. The gang broke up in 1721, when Gabriel Tomkins was chased and eventually caught at the village of Nutley near Uckfield. Without their leader the gang simply slipped back into their traditional farming methods as if nothing had happened in the intervening years. The image of the smuggler as portrayed in films is of the lovable scoundrel who is always kind to the ladies and hard, but at least fair, to the men he encounters. The Mayfield Gang seem to support this nostalgic, cinematic view. Over the next fifteen years, gangs came and went, but around 1735, a new force appeared in the area and the mood changed.

In sharp contrast to their predecessors, the Hawkhurst Gang operated on a scale and used methods that brought fear to the local population. Their area of operation and their sphere of influence spread along the coast all the way from Herne Bay on the north Kent coast to Poole in the west, a distance equating to

The Oak and Ivy Inn, which was the main base in Hawkhurst for the smuggling gang.

around 250 miles of coastline. Two brothers, Arthur and William Gray, led the Hawkhurst Gang, but two other influential members were another pair of brothers, Thomas and George Kingsmill, both of whom lived in Goudhurst. The gang consisted of at least 150 regular members, though reports state that as many as 500 men, most of them with horses, could be called on at an hour's notice if required.

As the wealth and influence of the Hawkhurst Gang grew, so did its reputation for brutality. They ruled their area with such repression that they would openly enter villages, breaking into houses and bullying the occupants into parting with their possessions. Women and children were also abused and any who resisted were either beaten to death or simply disappeared. An example of this brutality is that perpetrated upon a Mr Ballard, a gentleman passing through Goudhurst on his way home to Tunbridge Wells. He was attacked in the street at Goudhurst and robbed of £39, his watch and ring before being soundly beaten. Later he was carried home but died some four hours after his return as a result of his wounds.

It is a well-known story in Rye that the Hawkhurst Gang were so brazen that the leaders would openly sit at the Mermaid Inn with their loaded pistols on the tables before them. On one occasion, twenty or so members of the gang wandered from the Mermaid to another Rye inn, the Red Lion, where they fired their pistols into the ceiling to frighten the locals, one of whom, a James Marshall, took more than a passing interest in the event. It is not known what happened to James Marshall after the Hawkhurst Gang removed him from the Red Lion; it seems that his name was merely added to the list of those already missing.

The Hawkhurst Gang was no less fearsome with its own kind. In 1746 a dispute occurred between them and the Wingham Gang, who were based near Canterbury. Halfway through the unloading of a consignment of tea at Sandwich in Kent, the Wingham Gang decided that they would not wait for the unloading to be completed and made off with more than their fair share, leaving the Hawkhurst Gang to deal with any interference from the authorities. The Hawkhurst Gang were furious at the risk they had incurred and the share of the tea that they had lost. A few days later the Hawkhurst Gang, fully armed, returned to Wingham to teach their former collaborators a lesson. It is reported that as many as seven of the Wingham Gang were wounded, though none appear to have been killed, and the Hawkhurst Gang recovered some of their tea and seized forty horses as recompense for their troubles.

However, the Hawkhurst Gang was not without its own setbacks. In 1740 George Chapman was one of a number of the gang who were cornered by the revenue at Silver Hill, a high point halfway between the villages of Hurst Green and Robertsbridge. One of the revenue officers, a Thomas Carswell, was shot and killed while trying to arrest the smugglers. George Chapman was found guilty of the murder and hanged in his home village of Hurst Green. However, such was the profit to be made from smuggling that there were always more men willing to join the gang, replacing any who had been 'lost' to the authorities or the hangman's noose. The website for the history of Kent (www.historic-kent.co.uk) suggests that, through smuggling, a farm labourer could earn in one night more than a week's farm wages, and the seduction by the smuggling gangs of the land labourers severely disrupted the whole local farm economy.

The greatest setback to afflict the Hawkhurst Gang, which eventually led to their downfall, began in March 1747, when William Sturt returned to his home in Goudhurst. Sturt was apparently an ex-corporal in the army and he was horrified at the way in which the villagers were left to the mercy of this gang of smugglers. Accordingly, he roused the villagers and asked them to stand up to this gang once and for all. Together they swore articles on 17 April and at once Sturt, using all of his military experience, began training the men. It was not long, however, before the Hawkhurst Gang got news of the resistance, but they were so confident of their success that they sent the informer that they had captured back to Goudhurst with a verbal message for Sturt, outlining what the gang intended to do. The message stated that for having the audacity to try and repulse further adventures by the gang, George Kingsmill would go and gather his whole gang together, well over a hundred strong, and bring them at a predetermined time to plunder every house, murder every soul within, and finally burn the place to the ground. When the Hawkhurst Gang had finished, Goudhurst would be no more. Kingsmill even gave the date and time at which they would carry out this sack of the village – 12 noon on 21 April.

RECONSTRUCTING THE BATTLE

Given the reputation of the Hawkhurst Gang, this was no idle threat, but Sturt was not a man to be shaken. Sturt must also have had great confidence in his own ability and a great deal of courage, because he must have realised that if things went against him and his militia, the Kingsmill brothers would undoubtedly carry out their threat, and Goudhurst would be destroyed. It is not clear how long Sturt had to prepare his militia. The articles had been sworn on 17 April and the battle was fought on the 21st, a period of four days. However,

SMUGGLING

Smuggling must come a close second to the claim of prostitution to be the oldest profession and, as today's television news programmes show, smuggling is as rife now as it has ever been in the past. Though some of the goods being smuggled may have changed, the majority, alcohol, narcotics and people, have been consistently smuggled, not only in Britain but also throughout the world.

In Britain, smuggling first began in earnest in about 1300. This was as a direct result of a new custom duty that Edward I had placed on the export of wool. Wool was the 'oil' of medieval trade, as the enclosure of the land discussed in chapter three, 'Norwich', clearly shows. Until Edward introduced this custom duty, all trade both in and out of England had been tax-free. But the King found that his new duty raised plenty of money for the exchequer, allowing him to fund his continuing wars in France. Accordingly, each time the duty went up, so did the amount of smuggling. By 1357 it can be seen that courts were beginning to try those arrested for smuggling goods through the unlicensed ports. In 1614 the export of any wool was made illegal and this was followed in 1661 by the introduction of a mandatory death sentence for anyone caught doing so. This led to a military escalation among the smugglers as they started to arm themselves and to buy or build their own ships, complete with cannon. The results of this can be clearly seen from the trade records for Calais in 1670, which show that a staggering 20,000 packs of wool were being annually imported from England.

The eighteenth century was the 'Golden Age' of British smuggling, that 'growing night-time trade', as one customs officer put it. There are two principal reasons for the dramatic increase in smuggling from 1700 onwards. First, the century was one of almost continual European warfare. It opened with the War of the Spanish Succession (1700–13), followed in turn by the War of the Polish Succession (1733–5), the War of Jenkins' Ear (1739), the War of the Austrian Succession (1740–8), the Seven Years War (1756–63), the War of American Independence (1776–83), the French Revolutionary Wars (1793–7) and finally the Napoleonic Wars (1797–1815). Given the amount of time, money and resources that was being put into expanding the British navy to support what had by 1763 become a large empire following the Treaty of Paris, it is clear that there was a dearth of funds left to deal with the growing scourge of smuggling at home. The second reason is that the prosperity in Britain in the second half of the century, founded on the trade developing from Britain's expanding empire and the new markets abroad, established a demand for goods for which people were prepared to pay the minimum rather than the going rate. If this meant that some underhand dealing had to be done, then so be it. Even if a gang was brought to trial, often the evidence was weak, and locals were either in the gang or afraid to speak up because of the fear of reprisals against them or their family. The local landowners, judges, clergy and even the local gentry were often involved commercially.

It seems that no one was immune from involvement, as the case involving Sir William Courtenay, the Member of Parliament for Canterbury, clearly illustrates. Sir William Courtenay gave evidence at the trial of a smuggler accused of being caught in the act of unloading illegal cargo at sea, in order not to be caught with the aforesaid cargo on board his vessel. Yet the revenue cutter managed to close and capture the smuggler and his vessel, having passed the bobbing barrels of cargo during the chase. At the trial Sir William stated under oath that he had witnessed the whole event from a vantage point upon the foreland and that the barrels had been there long before either vessel had appeared! Fortunately for the sake of justice the prosecution was able to prove that at the time of the incident Sir William Courtenay had been attending church some miles away. This perjury clearly shows how high the corruption of smugglers' gold could reach, though suffice it to say that this corrupt 'worthy' fell from grace to end his days in an asylum.

The basic economic law of supply and demand applied most clearly in Britain in the eighteenth century. The demand for contraband was high and as the risks declined, so the smuggling trade grew. The commonest items smuggled were tobacco, spirits, wine, silk, handkerchiefs, hats, live animals, people, snuff, playing cards and, on occasion, ships themselves. The gangs that conducted the smuggling

A smuggler brazenly loads his pistol in the street, a common eighteenth-century sight in Kent. *(Geoff Buxton)*

were slick organisations with intelligent people leading them. As many television series show, smugglers used caves and other natural features of the landscape to conceal their contraband from the prying eyes of the coastguards. But there were more subtle ways that the smugglers employed. Firstly, all the cargo would be shipped in small casks, specially designed so that each one was small enough for a man to carry. These casks were also small enough to be slung on donkeys or packhorses and to be slipped through windows or rock clefts through which normal barrels would not fit. Secondly, the smugglers developed a series of tricks that enabled the cargo to be hidden. These included covering the barrels in a wash of plaster of paris and leaving them stacked against the foot of a cliff above the tide line, so that they could not be seen from the sea because they looked just like the cliff face. Cargo was often weighted down and roped along the sea bed, or a lake, like a line of lobster pots, which could be collected by the gang when 'the coast was clear'. Tricks to hide cargo on board a ship included hollow masts or hollow oars; ships with two hulls (one inside the other, with cargo in-between); lengths of timber which were split and hollowed and filled with contraband before being bolted back together; and even vessels with false floors with the ballast covering the higher floor, leaving the goods concealed on the real floor below. The customs men today probably encounter many such subtleties in their continuing battle to thwart the smuggler while endeavouring to ensure that the exchequer is not cheated.

at least one day must have been lost because an informer had to tell the Hawkhurst Gang and then return to the village with the challenge from George Kingsmill, stating when the gang would attack. It seems most likely, given what Sturt achieved, that he must have had at least two days' notice, because in what little time was available Sturt accomplished through his militia a series of defences that any modern military engineer would be proud of.

The tower of the church with its crenellated wall and uninterrupted views was where Sturt made his headquarters. Firstly, every available firearm and ounce of gunpowder was rounded up. Secondly, there was clearly a lack of ammunition, because lead had to be procured from around the village to be cast into musket balls, a task that Sturt now allocated to some of his new recruits. While the weapons and ammunition were being assembled, a series of trenches and barricades were constructed, blocking all of the roads into the village and ensuring that there was an outer ring of defences, which would have to be breached before the church could be assaulted. Next, Sturt surveyed the outskirts of the village and set up observation posts in every concealable vantage point; the upper storeys of barns, windmills, farmhouses and large trees were all used, to ensure that the village would not be taken by surprise, no matter which direction the smugglers came from. It is reasonable to assume that Sturt placed his experienced militia, those who already knew how to fire a musket, in these observation posts, because once the firearms and ammunition were assembled, Sturt, with the rest of the time available, trained these raw villagers both how to fight and how to shoot. As the time appointed by the smugglers approached, Sturt ensured that all the women and children were locked in the church for security.

There is some debate as to the exact time that the Hawkhurst Gang appeared up Back Lane, parallel to the High Street. Some reports state that it was precisely at noon, others that it was nearly five o'clock, though the latter is considered to be the most likely. Most of the smugglers were on horseback, riding with shirtsleeves flapping and handkerchiefs tied around their heads, presumably for recognition purposes once the battle started. Each smuggler was armed either with a musket or a carbine, and all carried at least a brace of pistols and a sword.

Seeing the barricade blocking the gang's way, George Kingsmill rode up to it and shouted that he was not concerned about the village's attempts to hinder him. He had already killed no less than forty of His Majesty's soldiers or revenue officers, and staring at the Goudhurst militia before him, he said that he 'would be damned if he did not broil and eat four of their hearts for his supper' (tradition). Following this display of bravado, Kingsmill ordered his men forward to the attack.

Sturt had told his men to receive the first fire should a battle ensue, and bravely, and without falter, the militia let the smugglers come on. Getting close to the church wall and the barricade before them the smugglers let forth a volley at the militia and then charged. Amazingly not one militiaman fell. Sturt gave the order to reply and the militia's volley killed a smuggler outright and some others were wounded. The advancing gang now took cover behind any available object, tree, wall or hedge.

For almost an hour, a sporadic firefight raged, with casualties but no fatalities occurring on either side. Then George Kingsmill charged his horse towards the barricade at the top of the High Street and leapt over it, determined to get into the church, but he was shot dead as his horse leapt, his body staying in the saddle at first and then slowly falling at the church door. With one of their leaders killed, the stunned Hawkhurst Gang began to retreat in disarray and disperse across the fields away from the village. This retreat became a rout as the observers in their vantage points sent more shots at the smugglers as they fled, then with a signal from Sturt the militia from the village left their defensive

Goudhurst Church and churchyard, in which the majority of the fighting took place.

posts and joined in the pursuit. Of the 150 members of the Hawkhurst Gang who attacked Goudhurst, only two were killed, but others were wounded or captured. As examples to others, the bodies of George Kingsmill and Woollett were hung in gibbets outside George Kingsmill's father's house, in what is now known as Gore Lane, north of Goudhurst at 395 723.

Although they were weakened, this was not quite the end of the Hawkhurst Gang. While they left Goudhurst alone, the gang concentrated their work in Dorset and, having had a cargo confiscated by the customs officers, gathered their forces, broke into Poole Customs House and took their contraband back. This time, however, there were witnesses prepared to testify against the gang. When the Hawkhurst Gang dropped the leading witness and his escort down a dry well and then murdered them by dropping stones on them one at a time until they were crushed to death, there was uproar among the locals and the customs men alike. Eventually, the men responsible, including Thomas Kingsmill, were caught, and convicted at Chichester in January 1749. All six were hanged and then their bodies hung in chains, Thomas's being returned to Goudhurst to enable all to see that his terrible crimes had finally caught up with him.

The Battlefield Today

For the historian, the beauty of Goudhurst is not only in its picturesque streets and idyllic setting, but in the fact that the battlefield is still lying almost exactly as it was in 1747. The streets may be tarmacked instead of cobbled, stone and earth, but their location and the buildings that they pass remain the same. The church tower that was the dominant point of the battle stands so proud, a bastion that preserved, on that April day, the rights of free Englishmen to protect themselves, while at the same time the knave of the church below protected the sisters, wives and children of those men standing outside and facing probably the most dangerous day of their lives. On occasion a pageant is held in the church and churchyard to celebrate the villagers' victory over tyranny. Not only is Goudhurst unchanged, but also other places connected with the Hawkhurst Gang are still accessible to the public.

Exploring the Battle Site

Although the battle took place over a relatively small area, the visitor must travel in order to see all of the places connected with this event. Anyone just wishing to visit Goudhurst will be able to see everything on foot. Accordingly, as this is a most rewarding area to explore, I would recommend commencing the journey to the battle site with a visit to Rye. There are plenty of car parks scattered throughout the town. Once you are established, head for the High Street and then descend into the Mint, before turning up into Mermaid Street, where the Mermaid Inn will be found. It was this inn that the gang used to frequent when on business in Rye.

From Rye, take the A268 to Hawkhurst, some fifteen miles away. As you near the outskirts of the village, you will see on the right the Oak and Ivy Inn, which was the gang's local headquarters, where much of their planning was done; this is point A on the map. From Hawkhurst, take the A229 north towards Cranbrook. After almost two miles you will have risen uphill and as the road levels out you will find point B on the map, which is Tubs Lake. There is parking available in a pull-in just after the left turn of the staggered crossroads, which borders the lake. This overgrown and derelict-looking pond was one of the places used by the smugglers to secrete their casks on the way to London. From here the gang made their way to Goudhurst, but the eye-witness accounts about which route they took differ: it seems that they came from both sides of the village! It is the author's conclusion that the gang probably split up into two groups so as to approach the

WILLIAM STURT

The man who inspired the people to form their own militia and stand up to injustice was virtually unknown before his actions at Goudhurst. He was 'base' born in 1718 and then we know nothing about him until his name appears in the 15th Regiment of Foot in 1737. This regiment was ordered to Kent in April 1737 and in May of that year it was given instructions to assist civil magistrates and officers of the revenue in preventing owlers and smugglers from running goods. With these orders apparently came new uniforms. The regiment is recorded as recruiting while in Kent and it is most likely that William Sturt joined it at this time. Once recruiting was completed, the new men were sent to Canterbury to undergo basic training until they were 'perfected in their exercises'. In the spring of 1738 the regiment was moved to Wales, to both Swansea and Aberystwyth, again to support the civil authorities. This clearly shows how widespread smuggling was and how the government of the day was reacting to it. From Wales, the 15th was returned to the Southampton and Winchester areas before setting sail in August for the island of Dominica, where they arrived in December. This was a terrible ordeal for the British troops stationed there, and 90 per cent died, mostly of yellow fever. The remnants of the regiment arrived back in England at Plymouth on 21 December 1742. The regiment was so depleted by its last campaign that it would have needed to recruit extensively before it could again see service, which is presumably why nothing more is heard until August 1744, when it was back at Dover engaged in anti-smuggling activities. In July 1745 the regiment was sent to Ostend, but came back shortly after from Brussels, having almost been captured, to return to Kent, then Sussex, before being sent to Newcastle, Gateshead and Berwick. From September 1746 until March 1747 the regiment spent most of its time embarked on board ship waiting to invade Brittany, but this invasion never transpired. In the spring of 1747 orders were issued for more recruits and it seems that at this time William Sturt returned home. There are no records of him having attained any rank, though various records of the battle call him a corporal, a sergeant and even a lieutenant. Although he was unknown before Goudhurst, his skill, motivation and military strategy certainly gave his newly trained militia the courage and position from which to defeat the bravado and intimidation of their bullies. William Sturt deserves his place in English history.

Tubs Lake, so named because weighted barrels would sometimes bob to the surface, revealing the smugglers' hoard.

village from both the east (Iden Green) and the west (Tunbridge Wells) sides, giving themselves more of a chance to see what Sturt had prepared for them and also catching the militia from two sides should it come to a shoot-out.

From Tubs Lake continue on the A229, and then take a left turn onto the B2085 almost a mile further on. This runs for just over two miles before a T-junction appears, point C on the map. Turn left, joining the A262, which runs through Goudhurst. As you enter the village, the church will be seen ahead of you. Follow the road around, including a sharp bend in front of the church tower, and descend down the High Street, until a sign appears for a car park on the left, close to the village pond. Park here, point D on the map, and explore the rest of the village on foot. The church is located at point E on the map and is best approached by ascending the High Street.

CONCLUSIONS

Goudhurst is a most incredible event, arguably the last pitched battle on British soil, coming as it does a year after Culloden, although of course the numbers

Goudhurst High Street, at the top of which the Hawkhurst Gang found the militia manning barricades across the road.

involved were small when compared to the Jacobite Rebellion. The use of the militia, the street barricades, the snipers behind the windows and upon the church roof make it seem more akin to the hundreds of Hollywood Westerns than to a village in the Garden of England. Without the grit and determination of William Sturt, it is possible that the Hawkhurst Gang would have continued their illegal activities, submitting the south coast of England to a reign of terror for many more years. One must be thankful that this was a rare event in British history, and that such lawlessness declined once the Government realised just what a drain on the country's resources smuggling activities were. However, the Hawkhurst Gang and their actions have bequeathed to us the unique battle that was Goudhurst.

LOCAL ATTRACTIONS

Goudhurst is a pretty little village, served by a variety of shops, and there are tearooms and public houses at which refreshments can be obtained. The church, St Mary's, and its walled graveyard sit atop the hill and dominate the upper High Street. The unchanged nature of Goudhurst makes this a wonderful place to explore, and the visitor, ambling past the misshapen cottages and admiring the bowed roofs, is looking upon the buildings that witnessed the battle over 250 years ago. The nearest railway station is Tunbridge Wells. The tourist information centre is located at the Heritage Centre, Rye; telephone: 01797 226696.

St Mary's Church, Goudhurst is open to the public during daylight hours most days of the week. On weekends, between April and September, it is possible to gain access to the top of the church tower. There has been a church on the site since at least 1119, though given its prominent position it is likely that this has always been a sacred site. The vicar is Canon Peter Mackenzie, LLB MA MTh and he can be contacted at the Vicarage, Back Lane, Goudhurst, by telephone on 01580 211332, or by email at canonmack@talk21.com.

Hawkhurst is one of the largest villages in Kent and gave its name to the gang that disintegrated at the battle of Goudhurst. So wealthy did the Hawkhurst Gang become that some of the houses, shops and inns that form part of the colonnade on Highgate Hill, and some of those houses that radiate out towards Rye, Pipsden and Flimwell, were built and owned by them. The headquarters of the gang was the Oak and Ivy Inn, which is still a public house today and lies on the eastern edge of the village on the road to Rye.

Rye was one of the original 'Cinque Ports' and was a vital port until the estuary slowly silted up. Today the town is well serviced by a variety of shops and there are numerous places to eat and stay. As well as a good selection of normal high street names, there are many book and antique shops, including some that sell militaria from Rye's past. This is also the home of the fictional smuggler Captain Pugwash, whose author, John Ryan, still resides in the town. Since many of its thoroughfares are narrow and some are still cobbled, it is not difficult to imagine the smugglers and their contraband moving through the town.

Bibliography

As the reader will appreciate, the written information on some battles is very sparse, while on others, particularly those from the English Civil War onwards, there is abundant material, and in some cases sources can be quite contradictory to one another. This can be a result of misinterpretation of an event or deliberately manipulating the facts to suit the recipient; propaganda is not just a twentieth-century phenomenon. Accordingly, I have based my interpretation of the battles within this book not only on the written material available but most importantly on the site evidence, using my visits and examination of the relevant topography to see for myself where the relevant action battles are most likely to have taken place. I have not listed specific websites that have been used to confirm details that are known by locals as 'tradition'; there are simply so many for each battle, each conveying much the same information, but the problem encountered on many of these websites is the lack of references for their source data, and it is difficult to quote them without knowing their source. If a specific website has been used, it is accredited in the text of the relevant chapter.

SPECIFIC BIBLIOGRAPHY

BUTTINGTON – 893

The Anglo-Saxon Chronicle, tr. D. Whitelock, Eyre & Spottiswoode, 1961
Archaeologia Cambrensis 28, 1873
Durham, K. *Viking Longship*, New Vanguard Series, No. 47, Osprey, 2002
Froud, C. *Dark Age Warfare Army Lists 475–1000 AD: The Fourth Book of Hosts*, privately published, 1998
Heath, I. *Armies of the Dark Ages*, Wargames Research Group, 1980
——. *The Vikings*, Elite Series, No. 3, Osprey, 1985
Laing, L. and J. *Anglo-Saxon England*, Routledge & Kegan Paul, 1979
Nicholson, T.R. *The Viking*, Senate Publishing, 1999
Whitelock, D. *The Anglo-Saxon Chronicle, a Revised Translation*, Eyre & Spottiswoode, 1961
Wise, T. *Saxon, Viking and Norman*, Men-at-Arms Series, No. 85, Osprey, 1979
Wood, M. *In Search of the Dark Ages*, BBC, 1981

ST ALBANS – 1455

Ashdown, C. *The Battles and Battlefields of Saint Albans, 1455–1461*, no date
Featherstone, D. *Wargames through the Ages*, Stanley Paul, 1974, vol. 2

Froud, C. *Medieval Warfare Army Lists 1300–1500 AD: The Sixth Book of Hosts*, privately published, 1999

Haigh, P. *The Military Campaigns of the Wars of the Roses*, Bramley Books, 1995

Heath, I. *Armies of the Middle Ages*, Wargames Research Group, 1982, vol. 1

Wise, T. *The Wars of the Roses*, Men-at-Arms Series, No. 145, Osprey, 1983

NORWICH – 1549

Bindoff, S.T. *Kett's Rebellion 1549*, Historical Association, 1949

Cornish, P. *Henry VIII's Army*, Men-at-Arms Series, No. 191, Osprey, 1987

Gush, G. *Army Lists 1420–1700*, Wargames Research Group, 1984

Hoare, A. and A. *On the Trail of Robert Kett of Wymondham*, privately published, 1996

Miller, D. *The Swiss at War 1300–1500*, Men-at-Arms Series, no number, Osprey, 1979

——. *The Landsknechts*, Men-at-Arms Series, No. 58, Osprey, 1980

Newark, T. *War in Britain*, Grafton, 2002

POWICK BRIDGE TO STOW-ON-THE-WOLD – BATTLES OF THE ENGLISH CIVIL WAR – 1642–6

Adair, J. *By the Sword Divided*, Century, 1983

Archaeologia Cambrensis 36, 1881

Archaeologia Cambrensis: The Castle of Montgomery, combined edition, J.E. Tomley, no date

Asquith, S. *The New Model Army 1645–1660*, Men-at-Arms Series, No. 110, Osprey, 1981

Baker, A. *A Battlefield Atlas of the English Civil War*, Ian Allan, 1986

Buchan, J. *Montrose,* Thomas Nelson and Sons, 1928

Chapman, G. *The Siege of Lyme Regis*, Axminster Printing Co., 1982

Clarke, N.J. *The Book of the Cobb*, Cobblyme Publications, 2003

Emberton, W. *The English Civil War Day by Day*, Stroud, Sutton, 1997

Evans, D. *Montgomery 1644*, St Idloes Press, no date

Field, R. *Stow on the Wold 1646*, no date

Gush, G. *Army Lists 1420–1700*, Wargames Research Group, 1984

Gush, G. and Windrow, M. *The English Civil War*, Airfix Magazine Guide 28, Patrick Stephens, 1978

Haythornthwaite, P. *The English Civil War 1642–1651*, London, Guild Publishing, 1983

Hill, J.M. *Celtic Warfare 1595–1763*, John Donald, 1986

Reid, S. *Scots Armies of the English Civil Wars*, Men-at-Arms Series, No. 331, Osprey, 1999

Roberts, K. *Soldiers of the English Civil Wars (1): Infantry*, Elite Series, No. 25, Osprey, 1989

Tennant, P. *The Civil War in Stratford on Avon*, Alan Sutton, 1996

Tincey, J. *Soldiers of the English Civil Wars (2): Cavalry*, Elite Series, No. 27, Osprey, 1989

Verney, P. *The Standard Bearer*, Hutchinson, 1963

Wedgwood, C.V. *The King's Peace*, Collins, 1955

——. *The King's War*, Collins, 1958

Young, P. and Emberton, W. *Sieges of the Great Civil War*, Bell, 1978

Young, P. and Holmes, R. *The English Civil War*, Eyre Methuen, 1974

KILLIECRANKIE – 1689

Barthorp, M. *The Jacobite Rebellions, 1689–1745*, Men-at-Arms Series, No. 18, Osprey, 1982

Ede-Borrett, S. *The Army of James II*, Raider Games, 1987

Hill, J.M. *Celtic Warfare 1595–1763*, John Donald, 1986

Killiecrankie, National Trust for Scotland guide, 2004

Reid, S. *Highlander*, Publishing News Ltd, 2000

Sinclair Stevenson, C. *Inglorious Rebellion*, Hamish Hamilton, 1971

GOUDHURST – 1747

Douch, J. *The Wicked Trade*, Crabwell Productions, no date

Nicholls, O.E. *Honest Thieves*, Heinemann, no date

Phillipson, D. *Smuggling: A History 1700–1900*, David & Charles, no date

Williams, N. *Contraband Cargoes*, Longman, no date

GENERAL BIBLIOGRAPHY

Burne, A.H. *The Battlefields of England*, Greenhill, 1996

Carter, G. *Outlines of English History*, Wardlock, 1984

Davis, P.R. *Castles of the Welsh Princes*, Christopher Davies, 1988

Duke Henry Plantagenet (ed.). *Call to Arms*, Re-enacting Directory 2004/5, Beta Print, 2004

Fairbairn, N. *A Traveller's Guide to the Battlefields of Britain*, Evans Brothers, 1983

Funcken, L. and F. *Arms and Uniforms, Ancient Egypt to the 18th Century*, Wardlock, 1972

——. *Arms and Uniforms, The Age of Chivalry, Part 1*, Wardlock, 1980

——. *Arms and Uniforms, The Age of Chivalry, Part 2*, Wardlock, 1981

——. *Arms and Uniforms, The Age of Chivalry, Part 3*, Wardlock, 1982

Guest, K. and D. *British Battles*, HarperCollins, 1996

Harrison, I. *British Battles*, HarperCollins, 2002

Hill, J.M. *Celtic Warfare 1595–1763*, John Donald, 1986

Hobbes, N. *Essential Militaria*, Atlantic Books, 2003

Kinross, J. *The Battlefields of Britain*, David & Charles, 1979

——. *Discovering Battlefields of England and Scotland*, Shire, 2004

Low, S.J. and Pulling, F.S. *The Dictionary of English History*, Cassell, 1911

Matthews, R. *England versus Scotland*, Pen and Sword, 2003

Smurthwaite, D. *The Complete Guide to the Battlefields of Britain*, Mermaid Books, 1984

Warner, P. *Famous Battles of the Midlands*, Fontana/Collins, 1976

——. *Famous Welsh Battles*, Fontana, 1977

Index

Abbot of St Albans 19, 22, 24, 27
All Saints Church 10
Anglo-Saxon Chronicle 1, 5, 8, 13, 15
Archaeologia Cambrensis 1, 8, 10, 91, 92
Argyll, Marquis of 102, 106
Astley, Sir Jacob 115, 117, 118, 121–3, 125–7

battles
    Buttington 1–16
    Clifton Moor 134
    Culloden 134, 159
    Dunbar 62, 93
    Falkirk 134
    Goudhurst 147–61
    Inverlochy 99–114
    Killiecrankie 129–46
    Langport 115
    Lyme 67–82, 95
    Marston Moor 64, 73
    Montgomery 83–97
    Naseby 64, 73, 89, 96, 115
    Newburn Ford 57
    Norwich 31–49, 87, 152
    Philiphaugh 109, 115
    Pinkie 32
    Powick Bridge 51–66, 73, 88
    Prestonpans 134
    Rowton Heath 115, 117
    St Albans 17–30
    Sedgemoor 129, 131
    Stow-on-the-Wold 115–27
    Worcester 61–3, 93
Bennett's Gate 39
Bishop's Gate 32, 38, 39, 42, 44, 48
Blair Atholl (inc. Blair Castle) 99, 123, 132, 133, 140, 143, 145
Blake, Robert 69, 71, 76, 81
Brereton, Sir William 87, 91, 92, 119, 121, 123, 125
Bristol 67, 89
Brown, Colonel 53, 54, 58, 60, 61, 63
Buchan, John 102, 103, 105–7, 109, 112
Buckingham, Duke of 19, 22, 23
Buttington, battle of 1–16
Byron, Lord 90–2, 96

Campbell, Clan 102, 105, 106, 108, 110
Campbell, Sir Duncan 106, 110, 111
Cannon, Colonel 140, 145
Canterbury 150, 153
Charles I, King 51, 53, 56–8, 62, 67, 83, 89, 93, 99, 104, 105, 115, 117, 120, 124, 126, 127
Charles II, King 62, 63, 66, 93, 104, 120
Charlie, Bonnie Prince 134
Charmouth 76, 77
Chester 13, 53, 86, 115
Clifton Moor, battle of 134
Cobb, the 68, 69, 71, 77–9, 81, 82
Coire Choille (inc. Farm) 100–2, 105, 111
Cow Tower 44, 45, 48
Cow, Mayor 36–8, 44
Creag a'Chail 101, 103, 107, 112
Creag Eallaich 130, 133, 138, 141, 144
Cromwell, Oliver 62–4, 73, 93, 127
Culloden, battle of 134, 159

Davey's Fort 71, 72, 77, 80
Devil's Hole 84, 94, 95
Donnington 116–18, 121–3, 125–7
Dunbar, battle of 62, 93
Dundee, 'Bonnie', Viscount 129, 131–3, 136–8, 140, 141, 144, 145
Dunfermline, Earl of 130, 138, 140, 144
Dunkeld 133, 140
Dussindale 41, 43, 44

Edward I, King 152
Edward VI, King 31, 32, 34, 38, 48
Essex, Robert Devereux, Earl of 51, 53, 54, 58, 73, 76, 89, 124

Fairfax, Sir Thomas 62, 89, 125, 142
Fairfax, Sir William 87, 91, 92
Falkirk, battle of 134
Field, Roy 118–22
Fiennes, Nathaniel 54, 58
Flowerdew, John 33, 35
Fort William 99, 100, 102, 107, 112–14

Goudhurst, battle of 147–61

Hawkhurst 148, 157, 161
Hawkhurst Gang 147, 149–51, 154–7, 160, 161
Henry VI, King 17, 19–21, 24, 26, 29
Henry VIII, King 31, 34, 38, 46
Herbert, Lord Edward 86
Hesilrige, Sir Arthur 58, 73, 124

Inverlochy, battle of 99–114

James I (VI of Scotland), King 56–8
James II (VII of Scotland), King 129, 131, 134, 145

Kett, Robert 33–9, 42, 43, 48, 49
Kett, William 47
Kett's Oak 35, 46
Killiechonate 101, 103, 111
Killiecrankie, battle of 129–46
Kingsmill, George 150, 151, 154–6
Kingsmill, Thomas 150, 151, 156

Landsknechts 38–44, 48
Langport, battle of 115
Latimer, Hugh, Bishop of Worcester 34, 48
Leanachan (inc. House) 101, 103, 111–13
Loch Eil 103, 106, 107, 112
Loch Leven 105, 107
Loch Linnhe 99, 107, 110
London 17, 19, 58, 85, 89
Longborough 116, 118, 123, 125, 127
Ludlow 53, 64, 97
Lyme, battle of 67–82, 95

Mackay, Hugh, Major General 131–3, 136–40, 144
Margaret of Anjou 20, 26
Marston Moor, battle of 64, 73
Maurice, Prince 59, 67, 69–72, 74, 76, 77, 80, 81
Mayfield Gang 147, 149
Meall an t-Suidhe 100, 101, 103, 112
Meldrum, Sir John 87, 90, 91, 93, 95
Mermaid Inn 150
Middleton, Sir Thomas 85–7, 90
Montgomery, battle of and castle 83–97
Montrose, James Graham, Marquis of 89, 99, 101–13, 115, 120
Morgan, Colonel 118, 121, 123
Mousehold Heath 36–9, 41, 43, 44, 46–8
Mytton, Colonel Thomas 85–7, 90–2, 94

Naseby, battle of 64, 73, 89, 96, 115
Newburn Ford, battle of 57
Newtown 83, 86, 94
Northampton, William Parr, Marquess of 31, 38, 44, 48
Norwich 31–49, 82, 152
Norwich, battle of 31–49, 152

Oak and Ivy Inn 148, 149, 157
Offa's Dyke 1, 10, 90, 94, 95, 96
Ogilvie, Sir Thomas 106, 110
Oswestry 13, 85, 87
Oxford 104, 115, 117, 123

Palace Plain 38, 48
Philiphaugh, battle of 109, 115
Pinkie, battle of 32
Poole 149, 156
Powick Bridge, battle of 51–66, 73, 88
Powick Church 53, 60, 61
Powis Castle 2, 15
Prestonpans, battle of 134

Rownal 84, 94–6
Rowton Heath, battle of 115, 117
Roy Bridge 101–3, 110, 111
Rupert, Prince 51, 53–5, 58–60, 64, 73, 85–7, 124
Rye 150, 157, 161

St Albans, battle of 17–30
St Edward's Church, Stow 122, 126
Salisbury, Earl of 17, 20
Salt Bridge 84, 90, 91, 93–5
Sandys, Colonel 54, 55, 58, 63
Sedgemoor, battle of 129, 131
Shrewsbury 4, 11, 53, 85–7, 92, 97
Soldier's Leap 130, 143, 144, 146
Somerset, Sir Edmund Beaufort, Duke of 19, 20, 24, 28
Somerset, Edward Seymour, Duke of 31–3, 38, 48
Stow-on-the-Wold, battle of 115–27
Sturt, William 151, 154, 155, 158–60

Thirty Years War 51, 53, 108
Ton Man Ditch 22, 25, 27, 28
Torlundy 103, 112, 114
Tubs Lake 148, 157, 159
Tunbridge Wells 147, 149, 159, 161

Urrard House 130, 136, 137, 139, 141, 143, 144

Warwick, Earl of (in 1549) 38, 39, 41–4, 47, 48
Warwick, Earl of (in 1644) 69, 71, 76, 78, 81
Warwick, Richard Neville (in 1455, 'the Kingmaker'), Earl of 17, 23, 25, 28, 29
Welshpool 1, 2, 4, 5, 11, 13–16, 83, 85, 87, 94, 97
William of Orange 129, 131, 145
Wingham Gang 150
Worcester 34, 51–5, 60–5, 93
Worcester, battle of 61–3, 93
Wymondham 33, 35, 44, 46, 47

York, Richard Plantagenet, Duke of 17, 19, 20, 24, 29